D1015542

Praise for *The Future of Value*

"Sustainability is becoming an essential ingredient to high performance; leaders need to learn new skills to fashion sustainable and successful long-term careers for themselves. Lowitt's book will help current and aspiring leaders develop these new skills. *The Future of Value* is an essential read for any leader seeking to be highly successful today and tomorrow!"

—**Marshall Goldsmith,** author of the *New York Times* bestsellers *Mojo* and *What Got You Here Won't Get You There*

"*The Future of Value* makes a powerful connection between sustainability, strategy, and value creation with excellent examples and stories to illustrate its solid points. You will learn from this clear, concise, and useful guide to sustainable practices."

—**Andy Savitz,** author, *The Triple Bottom Line*

"Regardless of your stance on sustainability, *The Future of Value* is essential reading for innovative corporate leaders."

—**Tim Mohin,** director, corporate responsibility, Advanced Micro Devices

"This book is useful, well written, and timely. Sustainability has evolved from the periphery to the center of business attention, but we still have a lot to learn about how to embed issues like water and carbon into the bottom line. Lowitt explains how. He spent months interviewing leaders in the most advanced companies, and he shares what they are doing. We can take these lessons and put them to work. Lowitt's clear stories and frameworks are more useful than theories and more inspiring than sermons. I hope this book is widely read and put into practice because the earth will be a better place."

—**Hal Hamilton,** founder and codirector, Sustainable Food Lab

The Future
of Value

How Sustainability Creates Value
Through Competitive Differentiation

Eric Lowitt

Foreword by William Sarni

JOSSEY-BASS
A Wiley Imprint
www.josseybass.com

Published by Jossey-Bass
A Wiley Imprint
989 Market Street, San Francisco, CA 94103-1741—www.josseybass.com

Jossey-Bass books and products are available through most bookstores. To contact Jossey-Bass directly call our Customer Care Department within the U.S. at 800-956-7739, outside the U.S. at 317-572-3986, or fax 317-572-4002.

Jossey-Bass also publishes its books in a variety of electronic formats. Some content that appears in print may not be available in electronic books.

Library of Congress Cataloging-in-Publication Data
Lowitt, Eric.
 The future of value : how sustainability creates value through competitive differentiation/ Eric Lowitt ; foreword by William Sarni.
  p. cm.
 Includes bibliographical references and index.
 ISBN 978-1-118-07452-7 (hardback); ISBN 978-1-118-07823-5 (ebk);
ISBN 978-1-118-07824-2 (ebk); ISBN 978-1-118-07825-9 (ebk)
 1. Management—Environmental aspects. 2. Strategic planning—Environmental aspects. 3. Value. 4. Social responsibility of business. 5. Sustainable development. I. Title.
 HD30.255.L687 2011
 658.4'08—dc22

                                                         2011015808

Printed in the United States of America
FIRST EDITION
HB Printing   10 9 8 7 6 5 4 3 2 1

To Allegra and our children, Dana and Alex

Contents

Foreword

For one to understand the importance of *The Future of Value* we must look back a few years to when the notion of sustainability was just entering our lexicon.

"What is sustainability?"

"Why would I spend money on any of this if I don't have to?"

These were the common questions just a few years ago when the business value of sustainability was, at best, an attractive concept but one that could reference few, if any, qualitative or quantitative success stories. Despite this significant limitation, many held on to the belief that sustainability had real business value.

Those of us who were trying to build businesses around sustainability consulting services referred to the "Brundtland Commission"[1] definition of sustainability or the "triple bottom line" from John Elkington.[2] While the Brundtland definition was useful for framing an ethos ("Sustainable development is development that meets the needs of the present without compromising the ability of future generations to meet their own needs"), it could not be readily translated into a business strategy or actions (some might argue this point). The "triple bottom line" took us further but still not far enough. In my opinion, the value of sustainability for businesses is not about balancing economic and social performance with economic performance (again, some might argue this point). Instead it is about proactively managing environmental and social performance to drive economic performance (more in line with the Dow Jones Sustainability Index view of sustainability, www.sustainability-index.com).

Our passionate and, of course, rational arguments were not enough to compel most business leaders to embrace sustainability as a strategy. This all changed as the value of sustainability became clear and sustainability went mainstream.

Key articles articulating the value of sustainability emerged. Stuart L. Hart and Mark B. Milstein identified sustainability as a driver for the creative destruction of industries and innovation.[3] Sustainability was framed within the business thinking of economist Joseph Schumpeter to describe a process in which the old ways of doing things are destroyed and replaced by new ways. Continued refinement of our thinking resulted in a more explicit thesis that sustainability is now one of the *key* drivers of innovation for businesses.[4] Taking this further we now recognize that companies are internalizing externalities unheard of just a few years ago. To quote the authors of a recent article, "Companies have long prospered by ignoring what economists call externalities. Now they must learn to embrace them."[5]

This shift in business thinking about the value of sustainability is now consistently confirmed by surveys of "C-suite" business leaders. A survey in early 2011 by MIT *Sloan Management Review* clearly lays out the business value of sustainability and reflects the increase in spending on sustainability initiatives during a global economic recession (more than 50 percent of the survey participants).[6] The value of sustainability was cited as a driver for innovation, increasing intangible (brand) value, adding potential new revenue streams through new products and services and reduced costs due to material or waste efficiencies, access to new markets and *increased competitive advantage* (my emphasis).

The conclusion is straightforward: companies are spending more on, and realizing increased top-line and bottom-line value from, sustainability initiatives.

This leads me to why this book is important. It moves the dialogue to the next phase of how we view sustainability and provides increased rigor in evaluating the real value of sustainability. Not simply anecdotal evidence that sustainability has value—this book provides a critical view as to why sustainability *is now fully integrated into business strategy.*

Much has changed in a very short period of time. If you are running a business, sustainability is the *right business thing to do* instead of the right thing to do. There is almost no other alternative for businesses to thrive in today's highly competitive global marketplace. *The Future of Value* can help companies embed sustainability into their overall business strategy and be more competitive in the global marketplace.

July 2011   William Sarni
Denver, Colorado

Preface

Three events set me on the path to write this book. The first event traces its roots to a post office in Smithtown, New York. My dad, Dr. Michael Lowitt, a psychotherapist, had long been curious about the fate of "Dear Santa" letters sent by underprivileged children. One wintry day in the mid-1980s he went to the post office and learned about the existence of a stack of "Dear Santa" letters that had gone unread, let alone unanswered. He took a sample of these letters home and was deeply touched by their contents. Amid the raft of letters asking for video game systems and the like were a set of letters asking for the barest of necessities: food, clothes, warmth. A man with the biggest heart around, my dad sprung to action that day. He organized local businesses to donate these necessities of life. He personally answered hundreds of letters. And whatever needs weren't met through donations from others, he took care of himself. Hence the "Smithtown Holiday Project" was born. As a young boy I learned about the power of entrepreneurship, the benefits of giving, and perhaps most important, the meaning of creating value for other people.

The second event was a chance meeting in New York City in 1996. For context, the reader must know that I have always been fascinated by the art of crafting strategy. There's just *something* very cool about planning a path through competition to success. I started my first job out of college in 1996, working as a management consultant at what was then known as Andersen Consulting (long since known as Accenture). I was assigned to

Andersen's New York office. Since I had a modest amount of financial services experience from interning during college at Prudential Securities (retail brokerage) and then Merrill Lynch (bond trading), I joined Andersen's financial services industry practice, as part of the company's process competency group. My first gig was an internal project focused on populating the company's internal knowledge management system with best practices from the company's financial services projects. It was during this time I met a man who changed my life.

David Cohen is one of the most amazing people I've had the privilege to know. He has that rare combination of off-the-charts intelligence and go-out-of-his-way niceness. When we met, David was a partner in the company's financial services industry practice. He was regularly called upon by his peers to provide subject matter expertise in financial services, strategy, and process design. As the reader might suspect, David's office was lined with business books of all shapes and ages—a day spent in his office was a day spent with Michael Porter, Tom Davenport, Henry Mintzberg, Michael Hammer, Bruce Henderson, and Gary Hamel.

David took me under his wing. He lent me a new strategy book nearly every Monday with the unspoken agreement that I would read it and be prepared to discuss it with him shortly thereafter. I started with *The Discipline of Market Leaders* by Michael Treacy and Fred Wiersema. Then I read *Beyond the Hype* (Nitin Nohria), *The Death of Competition* (James Moore), and *Value Migration* (Adrian Slywotzky). Over three years David afforded me the luxury of access to more than 100 of these strategy books. Writing one has always been a closely held goal of mine.

Fate conspired with passion and fascination in November 2007. As a research fellow in Accenture's Institute for High Performance in Boston, I was responsible for leading a line of business research; at the time I was focused on the intricacies and drivers of customer loyalty. I had wanted to carve a niche in this field but frankly was struggling to find a large enough "white space." One night I received an email from Bob Thomas, director of the institute. He said that Mark Spelman, who was the managing partner of Accenture's Global Strategic Services consulting practice, wanted to develop a sustainability research program to support the company's new sustainability consulting practice. Mark had asked Bob if I was available to pitch in. I didn't need to be asked twice.

After two years of leading this line of inquiry, I left Accenture. Unsure what I wanted to do next, though fueled by a passion to further study the link between performance and sustainability, I set out to design a research program that would support a book that combined my sustainability, strategy, and value creation interests. I hope you enjoy reading this book.

The third event took place in 1994. I had the opportunity to study in Japan. I attended a university called Kansai Gaidai, located in a city called Hirakata, between Osaka and Kyoto. The university had a large base of exchange students from all regions of the world. Every day one could hear ten to twenty languages simultaneously spoken in a beautiful blend in the school's student lounge. One day I met a woman named Julie, who was from Kentucky. An avid reader, Julie had this ability to quickly look at someone and unearth a piercingly true insight. She looked at a poorly dressed, long-haired blond guy from New York and confidently predicted, "You are going to write a book someday." I don't know where Julie is these days; it's been more than fifteen years. But if you are out there, and somehow reading this, please know that you planted an idea that day. Thank you!

July 2011   Eric Lowitt
Needham, Massachusetts

Acknowledgments

Like any endeavor that requires great effort, this book is the result of the combined contributions of many individuals and institutions.

The Future of Value would not exist without the kindness of strangers turned friends. I often contacted sustainability and strategy practitioners "out of the blue." More than 80 percent of these folks not only responded but allowed me to interview them. In no particular order, my eternal gratitude goes out to Julie Bisinella at Australia & New Zealand Bank; Dan Cherian at Nike; Brian Larnerd and Lauren Garvey at Hitachi; Richard Verney and Michelle Hamm at Monadnock Paper; Santiago Gowland at Unilever; Lynnette McIntire and Ed Rogers at UPS; Tim Mohin at AMD; Ben Packard at Starbucks (and Ann Clark for helping facilitate the conversations); Edna Conway and Mandy Knotts at Cisco; Melissa Fifield, Renate Greelings, Kindley Lawlor Walsh, Jorge Perez-Olmo, and Lisa Carpenter at Gap Inc.; Adam Elman at Marks & Spencer; Amelia Knott at Centrica; Kevin Moss at BT Americas; Arlin Wasserman at Sodexo; Jean Sweeney and Heather Tansey at 3M; Cameron Schuster at Wesfarmers; Annie Lescroart at eBay; Julia King at GlaxoSmithKline; Frank Mantero at GE; Mark Schusterman, Paul Murray, and Gabe Wing at Herman Miller; Charles Ruffing and Chris Veronda at Kodak; Scott Carman and Jennifer Silberman at Hilton Worldwide; Mark Heintz at Deckers; Alison Presley at Travelocity; Dr. Eckhard Koch and Betsy Blicharz Arnone at BASF; and Peter DeBruin and Richard Pearl at State Street Global Advisors. Thank you everyone!

This book also would not exist if Accenture had not extended to me the opportunity to study the topic of sustainability. Thank you to Bob Thomas, Paul Nunes, Jeanne Harris, Mark Spelman, Terry Corby, David Light, Bruno Berthon, Peter Lacy, David Abood, Lisa LaPlant, and Jim Grimsley for believing in me and letting me study sustainability in a corporate setting. I had the privilege of working daily with very smart colleagues, who challenged my foundational thinking about sustainability. Among these colleagues (and friends) are Anna Caffrey, Judith Walls, Chi Pham, Chris Hilson, and especially John Glen.

Since I started this book right after leaving Accenture, I took great lengths to treat the Accenture content I produced as off limits for this book. Unfortunately that meant I needed to leave out content provided by preeminent sustainability companies and practitioners. That said, I want to thank Bonnie Nixon, Randy Boeller, and their colleagues at HP; Jennifer Mattes, Clay Nesler, and their colleagues at Johnson Controls; Roberta Barbieri and Carolyn Panzer at Diageo; and Caroline Angoorly, formerly of J. P. Morgan.

I am forever indebted to three colleagues in particular. Andy Hoffman took a sustainability neophyte and taught him both the literal meaning and ethos of sustainability. Will Sarni wholeheartedly encouraged me to write this book and not be satisfied with good when I should reach for great. David Cohen was instrumental in setting a young and inexperienced analyst on the path that ultimately led to this book. It would take several paragraphs to thank David for all he did for me. To Andy, Will, and David, please know I appreciate your friendship, your intellectual support, and your consistent willingness to help.

Cherie Potts and Pat Steffens at Wordworks deserve special attention. This sister team did yeoman's work quickly turning interviews into consistently flawless interview transcripts. Often

I submitted interview recordings to Cherie and Pat without advance warning. They always sent back verbatim transcripts within the shortest possible time frame, handled with the utmost confidentiality. Please consider yourselves partners in this book!

I spent most of 2010 with Deloitte Consulting LLP's Enterprise Sustainability practice. The experience of working with and learning from top-notch colleagues, including Karin Kin, David Linich, Chris Park, Julie Engerran, Eric Hespenheide, Peter Capozucca, Rachel Smeak, Amisha Parekh, and Joshua Rosenfield, is one I will always remember fondly. While with Deloitte Consulting LLP, I worked with several members of the UN Global Compact. Thank you to Ole Hansen, Gavin Power, Jerome Lavigne-Delville, and Georg Kell for allowing me to spend time with you and your organization.

Several advisers have become friends along the way. Among them are Mark McElroy at the Center for Sustainable Organizations, Asheen Pharnsey at SolidWorks, Joanne Lawrence at Hult International Business School, Gib Hedstrom at Hedstrom Associates, Noeleen Nunez at Net Impact at UMass Amherst, and Leslie Caplan at Leslie Caplan Consulting. Thank you for your kind support, your intellectual contributions, and your friendship.

This endeavor began with intensive research and ended with a book. To help get it there, I am indebted to my editor at Jossey-Bass, Kathe Sweeney, and her dedicated colleagues, including Dani Scoville, Alan Venable, Pam Suwinsky, Mary Garrett, and Jesse Wiley. Kathe championed this book from the outset; she stuck with this book project through various iterations and ultimately sharpened both the insights and the prose.

Finally, I owe my deepest gratitude to my family. In particular, my daughter Dana and son Alex, who frequently put up with me as I worked on this book. You two can now erase Daddy's book!

To my extended family, especially my parents, brother, sister-in-law, niece and nephews, and my in-laws, I owe my deep appreciation for your support, inspiration, and encouragement.

And to my wife, Allegra, whose love and never-ending support served as the foundation for this effort. I dedicate this book to you. Please know I am truly blessed to have you in my life—I am definitely the lucky one!

About the Author

Eric Lowitt is a strategy and sustainability consultant with fifteen years of management consulting and strategy experience in companies such as Accenture, Deloitte Consulting, and Fidelity Investments. He received his MBA from the Wharton School of Business. The author of numerous articles about sustainability, strategy, and value creation, Lowitt's work has been published in mainstream and practitioner journals such as *Forbes*, *Journal of Corporate Governance*, and *Business Strategy Review*. He and his wife live outside of Boston with their two young children.

The Future of Value

INTRODUCTION

Altruism is the enemy of sustainability.

The Future of Value is about a new way to create business value. *Business value* is defined as a return on investment from *stakeholders*, including shareholders, employees, and local community members. *Sustainable development*, coined by the Brundtland Commission as development that "meets the needs of the present without compromising the ability of future generations to meet their needs," has altered how companies create value.[1]

In this book, sustainability is not a synonym for "green" or altruism. By *sustainability* I mean a continuous, unwavering commitment that companies make to balance their financial returns with environmental impact and social equity investments. *Environmental impact* refers to things like companies' carbon emissions, water consumption, waste sent to landfill, and energy consumption. By *social equity investments*, I mean knowledge, technology, and financial and capital resources provided by companies to the local communities in which they operate.

Certain companies—*Sustainable Market Leaders*—have integrated a commitment to be sustainable into their short-, mid-, and long-term business decisions, investments, and activities. Sustainable Market Leaders stand out from their peers in three ways. First, their decision to integrate, not ignore, sustainability into daily business operations is leading to an ability to create increased top-line (revenue and brand value) and bottom-line (reduced expenses and reduced risks) value for their stakeholders.

The second way Sustainable Market Leaders are separating from their peers is by investing in their ability to change more quickly as needed. As we will see, business megatrends, such as sustainability, are now being initiated by stakeholders writ large, not solely by shareholders. There will be another megatrend all companies will need to deal with after sustainability. Given stakeholders' prominent role in both sparking and fueling the sustainability movement, it is reasonable to assume that stakeholders will play a significant role in the next megatrend after sustainability. Sustainable Market Leaders are beginning to trust and work with stakeholders and will gain insight into the next megatrend before their peers. As a result, these companies will start adjusting to the new megatrend's realities ahead of their competitors.

The reverse also holds true: companies that are ignoring the pursuit of sustainability are increasing the likelihood that they fail. One reason why is that these companies rely on a combination of altruism and "Do less harm" thinking to justify their sustainability initiatives. Such thinking can form a compelling argument for action once, maybe twice. But ultimately altruism won't convince business leaders to forever change how they make decisions, place investments, or launch activities.

In a way, this book is dedicated to these companies. By reading this book, those companies will be equipped to view integration of sustainability as a means to create new business value. *The Future of Value* reveals the steps Sustainable Market Leaders are taking to embrace sustainability as a new and powerful means to create value today and be more agile than their peers tomorrow. Interviews with executives at these extraordinary companies bring these imitable steps to life. (See Table I.1.)

Why This Book and Why Now?

We have entered a period of slowing growth worldwide. Competition is likely to increase as more and more companies from developing countries enter the global marketplace. The

Table I.1 Featured Sustainable Market Leaders

Organization	Region	Industry
Australia & New Zealand Bank	Asia and Oceania	Financial services
Hitachi	Asia and Oceania	Electronics
Wesfarmers	Asia and Oceania	Conglomerate
Aviva	Europe	Insurance
BT	Europe	Telecommunications
Centrica	Europe	Utilities
GlaxoSmithKline	Europe	Pharmaceuticals
Marks & Spencer	Europe	Retail
Sodexo	Europe	Food services
Unilever	Europe	Consumer products
3M	United States	Diversified technology
AMD	United States	Technology
Cisco	United States	Network and communications
DW Morgan	United States	Logistics
eBay	United States	Retail
Gap Inc.	United States	Retail and apparel
General Electric	United States	Diversified technology
Herman Miller	United States	Furniture
Hilton Worldwide	United States	Travel and leisure
Kodak	United States	Diversified technology
Monadnock Paper	United States	Commercial paper products
Nike	United States	Retail and apparel
Starbucks	United States	Food
Travelocity	United States	Travel and leisure
UPS	United States	Logistics

effects of the massive global recession will be felt for a very long time due to a drop in consumer trust of the private sector and government regulations intended to reduce the likelihood of systemic collapse. Companies are seeking ways to reduce expenses, build cash reserves, and make selective investments to capture growth.

Yet the world faces many pressing needs: dramatic food supply shortages, growing tension due to the expansion of the great divide between the haves and the have nots, and climate change, just to name a few. Against this backdrop of challenged growth, it is easy to understand why many companies are waiting for the government to take action before they invest in becoming sustainable.

The twelve months I have been working on this book— December 2009 to December 2010—have witnessed the failure of the Copenhagen talks to reach a binding global climate change agreement, followed by the U.S. Senate's failure to pass meaningful climate change legislation. Without legislation, companies will need a different reason to embrace sustainability. As numerous market-leading firms are demonstrating, traditional business rationale is standing in as this needed reason. Sustainable Market Leaders have adopted sustainability as a new lens through which to evaluate past business performance, current capabilities, and future investments. They are discovering that by committing to and then deeply ingraining the ethos of sustainability within their operations, they are able to create more value for their shareholders and other stakeholders alike.

Integration of sustainability by some but not all companies has led to changes in each of the balance of power within each of Michael Porter's Five Forces of Competition (discussed in Chapter Two). That is, Sustainable Market Leaders are shaping how their companies and their peers compete for revenue, for talent, and for the right to be viable over the long term. Companies that have not yet embarked on their sustainability journeys are being left behind. If this scenario plays out to an ultimate end state, many of these companies may be out-flanked to the point that their very survival is called into question.

A New Way of Thinking About Sustainability's Role in Value Creation

This book is based on a clear premise. Companies that embrace sustainability sharpen their strategies and strengthen their ability to execute, leading to value creation for stakeholders (see Figure I.1). That is, integrating sustainability into strategic-planning exercises helps companies identify new growth opportunities while reducing their exposure to legal, resource, and sociopolitical risk. In turn, sustainability leads companies to cast an even more critical eye toward both the efficacy and long-term viability of their value chain activities. This is how Sustainable Market Leaders create increased top-line (revenue and brand value) and bottom-line (reduced expenses and reduced risks) value for their stakeholders.

Figure I.1 Sustainability Equips Companies to Create Value

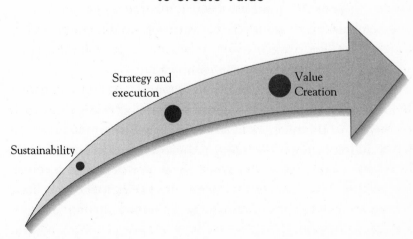

Strategy and execution

Value Creation

Sustainability

Why *You* Should Read This Book

Anyone who is interested in business value, competitive strategy—or sustainability more broadly—should read this book. Although there's something for anyone who cares about creating business value or achieving a state of sustainability, this book's findings have critical implications if you are . . .

- *A CEO or a small-, mid-, or large-size organization.* If you lead an organization of any size, your most pressing challenge is creating value every day. By reading this book, you'll see how applying the successful practices of Sustainable Market Leaders can help you dramatically increase your organization's ability to create value. But like many of the companies I studied, you may need to customize the lessons in this book to your specific situation. The book provides a starting point for thinking about sustainability not as altruism but as a path to sustained greatness as an organization.

- *A board member or similar individual within one or more organizations.* Board members are frequently queried about their companies' sustainability commitments and efforts. Given the myriad pulls on their time, and the relative freshness of this topic, more than a handful of board members fail to see a link between sustainability and value creation. For these board members, I recommend reading Chapter Three, which shows the variety of ways Sustainable Market Leaders are connecting sustainability with value creation. For board members who are well versed in the nuances of sustainability, I recommend thinking through Part Two of the book, which focuses on strategy and execution. These chapters will enable you to ask your chief executive officers savvy questions about their efforts to integrate sustainability for differentiation and value creation.

- *A leader at any level within an organization.* One of the differences between Sustainable Market Leaders and their peers is that Sustainable Market Leaders enlist the help of a wide range of managers to plot and carry out their sustainability efforts. You control resources that will be needed in order to execute your company's sustainability strategy. As a manager responsible for sustainability execution, you will be asked to shape employees' behaviors and roles to support your sustainability goals. I recommend carefully studying Chapters Six (sustainability implementation) and Seven (measuring and communicate sustainability performance) to guide you through your new responsibilities.

- *An employee at any level within an organization.* Employees have a unique and important role to play in their company's quest to become sustainable. Not only are you the front line for your company's sustainability efforts, but you are also a representative of society. This means that you help your company detect changes in society's expectations of corporations by providing feedback and suggestions to your company's sustainability managers. Chapter Eight is a must read for employees, as this chapter shows the impact employees at all levels can have on their company's ability to become sustainable.

- *A leader of a nonprofit.* Nongovernmental organizations (NGOs) are more and more frequently being asked to help improve companies' sustainability performance. But often these advisory relationships fail to live up to their potential because of some nonprofits lack deep business knowledge. The NGO or other nonprofit might recommend actions that make a company more environmentally or socially sustainable but at a great economic cost. The strategy formulation and implementation frameworks in Chapters Three, Four, and Five provide insights into the business "pain points" corporations face when making sustainability-related decisions.

- A *leader of a venture capital, private equity, investment bank, or other firm that provides a source of financial capital.* Sustainable Market Leaders are beginning to work collaboratively with their peers to bring about systemic change. For a variety of reasons, financial capital from a combination of internal *and* external sources is needed to finance these efforts. Venture capitalists and their investment peers control significant pools of liquidity, much of which is needed if industry is to ultimately become sustainable. These firms may be reluctant to place anything more than a small amount of their assets under management to back these sustainability endeavors. My hope is that this book will help convince these firms that an investment in sustainability is an investment that can bring more than just a tax deduction in return.

- A *sustainability consultant or adviser.* Many of the lessons contained within this book will require more professionals and more expertise than companies themselves have readily available. Consultants and advisors can use the frameworks throughout this book to help their clients benchmark, plan, and measure their sustainability investments and initiatives.

- An *academic.* Those who study sustainability have a special mandate. My research and methodology can only begin to make a deep, lasting connection among the separate but inseparable fields of sustainability, strategy, competitive differentiation, and value creation. My hope is that you will see my findings as a platform for future research—and I welcome your feedback.

- A *business and/or sustainability student preparing to enter or reenter the workforce.* Sustainability is a business imperative that will take decades to resolve. Today's students will be tomorrow's executives. To you falls perhaps the most difficult of all tasks. You might start your career full of purpose and motivation to create a better world. Never let go of this aspiration, even if your job temporarily takes you as far afield of your company's sustainability efforts as you possible can be. There is a component of any job that can contribute to the sustainability agenda. You just have to continually look for it and be willing to act when you find it. Ultimately you will be asked to make very painful decisions in the likely scenario that the actions we are taking today to become sustainable fall woefully short of what is needed. Never lose the courage of your conviction!

How to Read This Book

This book consists of two parts. The first part focuses on creating and protecting business value in a global market that is factoring sustainability into its expectations of organizations large and small alike. The second part provides readers with practical, Monday morning actions they can do to help strengthen their companies' strategy and performance through the integration of sustainability-oriented tasks and actions. Chapters Two through Nine offer diagnostic questions to push the readers' thinking about sustainability, strategy, and value creation.

Part One: How Sustainability Creates Value

Part One links a company's pursuit of sustainability with its ability to create value for stakeholders. Certain companies —Sustainable Market Leaders—employ sustainability as a means for competitive advantage. Their efforts are creating top-line (revenue and brand value) and bottom-line (reduced expenses and reduced risks) value for their stakeholders.

Chapter One: Sustainable Companies Are Market Leaders. Certain companies, called Sustainable Market Leaders, have integrated sustainability into their value creation efforts. In this chapter we learn about what separates these remarkable companies from their peers. In the process I describe the research methodology I developed to identify and learn more about Sustainable Market Leaders.

Chapter Two: Sustainable Market Leaders Compete on Sustainability. Sustainable Market Leaders are competing on sustainability. That is, these and other like-minded companies have carefully considered sustainability's impact on their competitive landscapes and adjusted their competitive strategies accordingly. Sustainability's impact on the competitive landscape is best viewed through the lens of Michael Porter's watershed Five Forces Model of Competition: suppliers, buyers, substitutes, new entrants, and industry rivalry. This chapter reveals the new algorithms in each force and enlivens this discussion with real-world mini-cases playing out across multiple industries. As the informed reader will discover, Sustainable Market Leaders are embracing sustainability not for altruistic purposes but for demonstrable, competitive differentiation. Their peers' decision to not adapt to sustainability's concerns and interests provides in itself another level of differentiation for Sustainable Market Leaders—a position far ahead of their peers along the learning curve of sustainable development.

Chapter Three: Competing on Sustainability Creates Value. Companies seeking progress along their sustainability journeys will need to marshal talent and financial capital, as well as senior management commitment, to fuel the adoption effort. Accomplishing this task requires the executive in charge of the sustainability proposal to demonstrate how sustainability can produce positive financial results. Sustainability executives must make the business case for embracing sustainability, as an investment in sustainability will reduce the investment pool for other worthy initiatives.

This chapter equips executives with the income statement– and balance sheet–rooted building blocks he or she will need to fashion a compelling business case. The case can be seen by exploring efforts Sustainable Market Leaders are making to grow revenue through innovation (and reverse innovation); lower costs; modernize their plant, property, and equipment; and nurture their portfolios of local licenses to operate.

Part Two: How to Create Value in Your Organization

Part Two shows how Sustainable Market Leaders have mainstreamed their sustainability management efforts. This part begins with an organized review of Sustainable Market Leaders' management practices. The resultant framework, which I call the CLEAR Model, is comprised of five pragmatic, timeless, and interlocked management practices, which will feel familiar to companies large and small, across all industries, operating in locations worldwide. Readers will learn about the top- and bottom-line improvement approaches, sustainability strategy crafting and governance structures, value chain activity adjustments, measurements, and engagement-driven renewal tactics employed by Sustainable Market Leaders.

My model is aided by the wide-scale adoption of frameworks that serve as springboards for the pursuit of sustainability. In particular is the Plan-Do-Check-Act (PDCA) model most often associated with W. Edwards Deming's work leading to the quality movement. Confident that the challenges and expectations that comprise the ethos of sustainability will evolve over time, I have taken the liberty of adding a step to the PDCA model—continuous renewal—and have adjusted language throughout (see Figure I.2). Sustainable Market Leaders are engaging stakeholders in dialogue to critique and improve their sustainability performance and management efforts. Part Two of this book

Figure I.2 The CLEAR Model: How to Embrace Sustainability and Maximize Stakeholder Value Creation

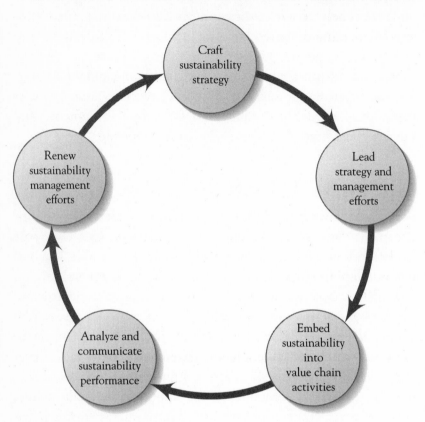

explores each step within this sustainability management framework.

Chapter Four: Crafting Sustainability Strategy. Once an executive gains organizational support to invest in and pursue sustainability, she would do well to concretize the company's sustainability interests into her company's competitive and corporate strategic-planning processes. That is because many of the adjustments required to become sustainable span both value creation processes (competitive strategy) and risk management processes (corporate strategy).

The first step in the sustainability plan formulation process is the completion of a holistic (and brutally honest) materiality assessment. Informed by the findings of this assessment, the company is then equipped to set goals, install and enact policies, and ultimately insert sustainability considerations into both strategy-making processes.

Chapter Five: Leading Strategy and Management Efforts. To assure stakeholders that their company takes this plan seriously, the Sustainable Market Leaders install a sustainability management and governance structure. Typically these structures include four components. The first is a central sustainability management team, usually consisting of between two and five employees dedicated full time to shaping and supporting the execution of their company's sustainability plans. The second component is a cross-department sustainability working group, including representatives from each business unit, function, and region. Usually these committees are counted on to develop sustainability plans, cut through bureaucratic red tape to pave the way to sustainability adoption, and lend their *gravitas* to the company's sustainability management efforts. The third component is a vehicle for stakeholder engagement, usually in the form of a stakeholder panel. These panels bring together senior executives with NGO, academic, and community leaders, usually between one to four times per year, to exchange views on the company's sustainability efforts. The fourth component is board-level oversight. Some companies have installed new board subcommittees, which meet quarterly to assess sustainability plans and progress. Other companies turn to their full boards for oversight by weaving sustainability into the other critical topics covered during board meetings.

Chapter Six: Embedding Sustainability into the Value Chain. All companies already have the fundamental processes and functions in place to embrace sustainability. Unlike the previous four imperatives that affected the way businesses create value (quality, business process reengineering, globalization, Internet) sustainability does not require expensive and disruptive change programs. Indeed, if we are to learn from Sustainable Market Leaders' efforts, then we can find comfort in the fact that the adjustments these companies have made are both easily understandable and imitable. This chapter shows how Sustainable Market Leaders are retooling their value chain activities to embrace sustainability within several functions, including

- Innovation
- Talent management
- Finance
- Business development
- Procurement and supply chain management

Chapter Seven: Analyzing and Communicating Performance. "What gets measured gets managed." Many of the world's most legendary companies have held this axiom at their core. Sustainable Market Leaders certainly do. They understand that significant pockets of public at writ view their commitment to sustainability with highly skeptical eyes. This skepticism is easy to understand. Individuals' trust in corporations to "do the right thing" is at a historic low. Sustainable Market Leaders realize the need to operate transparently as a key activity in their chain of actions intended to rebuild this trust. This chapter describes the various categories of measures Sustainable Market Leaders are employing. While measurement is crucial, measurement with communication is analogous to a tree falling in the forest unattended. This chapter also reveals the various methods (and reasons behind each method) Sustainable Market Leaders are using to communicate their progress (and missteps) to their range of stakeholders.

Chapter Eight: Renewing Sustainability Efforts. This chapter shows how companies are getting help to embrace sustainability from expected and unexpected people and organizations. Companies already have relationships with their managers, employees, communities, investors, analysts, suppliers, and even competitors. Market-leading companies are tapping into these relationships to get the help they need to embrace sustainability:

- Employees
- Customers and members of interested communities
- Value chain partners
- Competitors
- Nongovernmental organizations

In the process of reaching out to these obvious (employees) and not so obvious (competitors) resources, these companies are becoming stronger, more flexible, more relevant, and more aware. They are positioning themselves to perceive, understand, and respond to the next business imperative, regardless of the imperative's relationship to sustainability.

Chapter Nine: Keeping Sustainable and Agile. The concluding chapter explains why the modifications companies have made to integrate sustainability into business activities will lead to their ability to be more agile. Time was, business competition and innovation initiated new imperatives. The quality movement, which reached critical mass adoption among businesses in the 1980s and early 1990s, for example, was sparked by Japanese concerns to capture market share from their American peers by producing products that were more reliable.

Today society initiates imperatives. Environmentalists and social activists, their voices amplified by mass adoption of social media, have shaped and colored the sustainability movement. It is likely that society will shape and initiate the next imperative to affect business. Companies that work closely with society today will detect early signals of the next imperative before their peers. As a result, these companies—Sustainable Market Leaders—will adopt their activities to the next imperative's demands before their peers. Sustainable Market Leaders will be equipped to create value while their peers struggle to catch up.

Call to Action: Embrace Sustainability to Create Value Today and Tomorrow

While their peers have been wrestling with the decision to pursue sustainability, Sustainable Market Leaders have put themselves on a path to create more business value than their peers both today and tomorrow. Not only have these companies carved out competitive advantages today, but their swift and decisive actions have also positioned them for greater agility relative to the peers tomorrow. Their early adoption of sustainability has not only propelled their organizations up the learning curve faster and further afield of their peers, but their progressive actions have also led to relationships with the most visionary and influential stakeholders (leading NGOs, academics, local communities, and the like).

These stakeholder groups have both launched and colored the sustainability movement. These groups are likely to be the same influencers of the next imperative, regardless of its connection to sustainability. Sustainable Market Leaders have earned and secured access to these stakeholders' counsel. Whereas these companies will need only to traverse the next imperative's learning curve (with the benefit of counsel from the influencers of this subsequent imperative), their peers will need to work through at least two learning curves—sustainability (in part to earn relationships with these stakeholders) and the next imperative. So the additional activities adopted by Sustainable Market Leaders today will paradoxically make them faster than their peers tomorrow. Though sustainability's waters might evaporate, their collective impact will indeed be long lasting.

Part One

HOW SUSTAINABILITY CREATES VALUE

1

SUSTAINABLE COMPANIES ARE MARKET LEADERS

In the Introduction I promised to reveal how Sustainable Market Leaders are integrating sustainability into their daily activities in a way that enables them to create business value today and tomorrow. In this chapter I begin to prove this. I show how companies are separating from their peers by adopting the view that sustainability can lead to valuable competitive advantage.

Sustainability as Competitive Advantage: Three Examples

It is easy to understand why the *Wall Street Journal* chose the Bacara Resort as the setting for its inaugural Economics conference. Set between the Pacific Ocean and the Santa Ynez mountains, along the picturesque coastline of Santa Barbara, California, the resort offers breathtaking views. In a stunning combination of water, nature, and beach, the resort invites guests to relax, unwind, and rejuvenate.

Several well-known chief executive officers (CEOs) provided their perspective on balancing environmental, social, and economic pursuits—the three legs of the ethos commonly referred to as "sustainability." On March 12, 2008, perhaps the most enlightening view came at the beginning of the event. During the conference's first session, entitled "The Environment and the Business of Business," Jeff Immelt, General Electric's (GE) chairman and CEO, sat down on one of the white couches at the front of the room to present his views on sustainability.

During this talk to three hundred of the world's most influential executives, academics, and sustainability practitioners, Immelt described why he and GE were committed to the business of providing technology for the development of renewable energy: "I'm a capitalist and a businessman. I believe I can drive earnings and make money by working to create clean energy, water, and environmental solutions."[1]

Three years later, Immelt's conviction continues to be rewarded. GE's "ecomagination" line of environment-conscious products delivered $18 billion in revenue in 2009. In fact, since the launch of the ecomagination product line in 2005, GE has captured $70 billion in revenue. Looking forward, the company believes "ecomagination revenue will grow at twice the rate of total company revenue in the next five years, making ecomagination an even larger proportion of total company revenue."[2]

Our second example comes from several other scenic areas of the world.

Australia & New Zealand Banking Group (ANZ) has adopted the view that sustainability and core strategy are one and the same. The 175-plus-year-old Australian company is striving to become a super-regional bank with operations throughout Australia, New Zealand, Asia, and the Pacific. ANZ's approach to sustainability strategy is integral to its business strategy, brand, and goal to establish and build market leadership positions in several Asian countries.

ANZ's expansion into Cambodia provides an example of sustainability as market entry strategy. Cambodia has a population of 14 million people; yet only 500,000 have bank accounts. In 2009 the bank launched a wholly owned subsidiary called "Wing." Wing is a branchless banking service that enables customers to make person-to-person payments and conduct other retail banking transactions over their mobile phones. In so doing, Wing has made money transfers between people in metropolitan areas and rural areas more equitable, safe, and affordable, supporting goals to increase access to services and greater economic and social inclusion in rural parts of Cambodia. After its first year of operations, Wing already had about 100,000 customers.

This "bottom of the pyramid" service also provided valuable insights and experience for the development of "GoMoney™," for retail customers in Australia. According to Julie Bisinella, ANZ's head of corporate responsibility at the time (now ANZ's group head of culture and engagement), "Our efforts to respond to economic and social development issues and opportunities in Cambodia also informed the build out of an innovation that is now serving more profitable customers in Australia."

The travel industry provides our third example. The travel industry is instrumental in enabling people to rejuvenate at the Bacara Resort in California and experience the scenic beauty of Australia. But what enables competitive advantage in the U.S. online travel market? Conventional wisdom holds that advantage comes from lowest price, but lowest price is indefensible over the long haul.

Travelocity, the Dallas, Texas–based online travel service provider, is seeking to leverage its sustainability strategy to create business value in this intensely competitive market. In 2009 the company introduced its Green Hotel Directory, a part of its cause marketing program, "Travel for Good®." The Green Hotel Directory identifies third-party-verified "green hotels" and aims to serve environmentally conscious travelers.

What is the connection between the Green Hotel Directory and performance? While a few more quarters of data will be needed before findings can be confirmed, Travelocity is encouraged by early results. Year-over-year growth of third-party-certified green hotels outpaced peer hotel bookings by 65 percent during the first quarter of 2010 compared with the first quarter of 2009. Sensing an opportunity to develop competitive advantage based on the Travel for Good program, the company has begun to ramp up the program and now has flagged more than 2,500 properties that have been third-party verified as being "Eco-Friendly Hotels" on its main travel website.

Traditionally, companies have viewed sustainability either as a type of risk that needs to be managed or as a vehicle for altruism. That is, one or more of the challenges of climate change, resource depletion, social divides, and the like can disrupt these companies' ability to create business value. As a result of this shortsighted view, many companies have adopted the view that sustainability is some sort of "stakeholder-imposed" Gordian Knot: Become sustainable or maximize financial performance. They simply want to find ways to cut or otherwise "deal with" the knot, then move on to other more competitive matters.

The three market exemplars I've just described have adopted a different view. They see sustainability and financial performance as partners in growth and competitive differentiation. For GE, sustainability is instrumental to revenue growth. For ANZ Banking Group, sustainability provides the strategy for market entry. For Travelocity, early results suggest that sustainability can lead to brand differentiation. In so doing, these companies are demonstrating that their business strategies can be enhanced through the integration of their approach to sustainability.

Are Many Other Companies Also Competing on Sustainability?

In this book I distinguish between business competitive strategy and business corporate strategy. I rely on the watershed thinking of the strategy author, lecturer, and consultant Michael Raynor. In his seminal book, *The Strategy Paradox*, Raynor says that *competitive strategy* "is about creating and capturing value."[3] It is focused on short- and intermediate-term decisions taken to best position a company's products and services as the solutions of choice in the minds of target customers. As such, competitive strategy is crafted and employed by the business units.

By contrast, *corporate strategy* "may primarily be about the identification and management of strategic risk."[4] So corporate strategy entails risk assessments like "What happens if oil reaches

$200 per barrel, carbon is priced at $50 per ton, or an automotive fuel standard of 50 miles per gallon is reached and enacted globally?" As we will see throughout this book, employing sustainability in competitive strategy requires including sustainability issues separately in both competitive and corporate strategy processes; it also requires that competitive and corporate strategy-planning processes work jointly.

So: Are many companies making sustainability an essential component of competitive and corporate strategy, or are GE, ANZ Banking Group, and Travelocity exceptions to the general rule? One way to begin to answer this question is to count how many companies are taking some form of action to at least respond to, if not embrace, sustainability. Unfortunately there is no agreed-upon way of measuring a company's level of sustainability, no actual process for counting, that tells us how many companies are actively becoming sustainable. To build a proxy answer, let's review the number of companies that provide insights into their environmental and social sustainability thinking.

Regarding environmental impact, we look to the corporate response rate to the annual Carbon Disclosure Project (CDP) questionnaire. The CDP is a nonprofit entity that represents 475 institutional investors that collectively manage more than $55 trillion of assets on behalf of institutional and individual investors. According to the CDP, 82 percent of the five hundred companies that comprise the FTSE Global Equity Index Series filed answers to the CDP's 2009 annual questionnaire on climate change.

While many companies are participating in the world's pursuit of environmental sustainability, many more companies are not. The Carbon Disclosure Project 2009 questionnaire response rate varies by region; for example, while 82 percent of the Europe 300 responded, only 66 percent of the S&P500 companies answered the CDP's 2009 questionnaire. In addition to location differences, a company's size affected its likelihood of response. Specifically, smaller companies were less likely to respond. (I assume that suppliers to large companies are mainly small- or mid-cap companies.) Data from the CDP's 2009 Supply Chain Report suggests this group is either not willing or more likely not able to formally disclose facets of their environmental footprints: "The CDP Supply Chain Project invited 2,318 suppliers to complete a questionnaire created by the collective efforts of 34 member companies in 2008. Of those invited, 634 (27 percent) provided a response. Another 136 (6 percent) formally declined to participate. The remaining 1,548 (67 percent) did not log on or formally respond to CDP, although some suppliers indicated a willingness to respond in future years."[5]

As this data suggest, many large companies and a smaller but not insignificant number of smaller companies have begun to report their carbon emissions. While this step suggests that these companies intend to address the scope of their environmental footprint, it is not by itself much progress toward facing the broad range of issues of environmental sustainability.

Moving from environment to social equity, we can tally the number of companies that have signed the United Nations Global Compact (UN Global Compact). The UN Global Compact is a strategic policy initiative for businesses that are committed to aligning their operations and strategies with ten universally accepted principles in the areas of human rights, labor, environment, and anticorruption.[6] Currently the UN Global Compact lists more than 8,000 organizations as active participants, including more than 5,000 companies. The UN Global Compact notes that the group of active participants is growing at a rate of 1,200 annually.[7]

While the data presented suggest companies are taking steps to embrace environmental and social sustainability, they alone do not provide a satisfying answer to whether integration of sustainability can promote growth and competitive differentiation.

My Research into Sustainable Market Leaders

To better answer the question of link between sustainability and competitive differentiation, I analyzed every 2010 Global Fortune 500 company's sustainability strategy, governance, and stakeholder relationship efforts. I created a method to identify Sustainable Market Leaders (described in the Introduction of this book) from this list. For more information on this method, refer to Appendix A: Research Methodology.

The identification of Sustainable Market Leaders among the 2010 Global Fortune 500 helped me compile a list of companies to interview for this book. In total I conducted more than 100 interviews with sustainability, strategy, and finance experts at these companies. The interviews make up a core part of this book. I frequently rely on quotes and stories from these interviews to bring many insights and recommendations to life.

Research Findings

My research revealed several useful insights:

1. *Sustainability efforts are paving the way to growth, lower costs, innovations, and enhanced agility through relationships with suppliers, stakeholders, employees, and even competitors.* In addition to GE, ANZ Banking Group, and Travelocity, companies such as Unilever, United Parcel Service, Cisco, Nike, and Starbucks have made powerful linkages between their efforts to embrace sustainability and their ability to "move the needle" of financial performance in the short and long term.

2. *Sustainability has changed the terrain of competition among organizations.* Sustainability has been embraced by some, but by not all, companies within the 2010 Global Fortune 500. As a result, the terrain of competition has changed.

The most effective way to see this is to evaluate the new balances of power in each of Michael Porter's Five Forces of Competition: suppliers, buyers, substitutes, new entrants, and industry rivalry (discussed further in Chapter Two). For example, Sustainable Market Leaders are mandating that their suppliers adhere to a series of sustainability-oriented behaviors and activities. If these suppliers don't, they run the risk of losing their Sustainable Market Leaders' business. The same dynamic applies during the procurement process. Two identical vendors bid to supply a Sustainable Market Leader with commercial grade paper. All things being at or near equal, the vendor that can demonstrate an ongoing commitment to sustainability has a greater likelihood of earning this business.

3. *Because sustainability enhances their competitiveness, Sustainable Market Leaders have mainstreamed their sustainability management efforts.* That is, these companies have installed sustainability management and governance structures to push sustainability management from the purview of the few to the responsibility of the many. In particular, Sustainable Market Leaders tend to install small, centrally managed sustainability teams that then develop, influence, and rely on an internal network of peers across all departments to integrate sustainability throughout corporate strategies, business plans, and value chain activities. The company's sustainability efforts and plans are overseen at the board level, either by the board writ large or by a subcommittee equipped to govern sustainability efforts.

The Longevity and Agility of Sustainable Market Leaders

By labeling exemplars of sustainability management "Sustainable Market Leaders," I mean to call attention not just to sustainability in the narrow environmental and social respects but to the fact that typically these leading companies have *sustained themselves* longer than have others. Sustainable Market Leaders (the first-quartile set of Global Fortune 500 companies that appeared most frequently on the most widely accepted sustainability rankings) have existed, on average, twenty-one years longer than the companies in the next quartile down. (See Figure 1.1.)

My study suggests a possible explanation for these companies' extraordinary lengths of existence. When faced with a new imperative, in this case sustainability, these companies employ remarkably similar response approaches:

- First, they seek to understand the imperative in terms that are relevant to them: what the imperative's impact

Figure 1.1 Average Years in Business per Scored Sustainability Leadership Quartiles Within 2010 Global Fortune 500

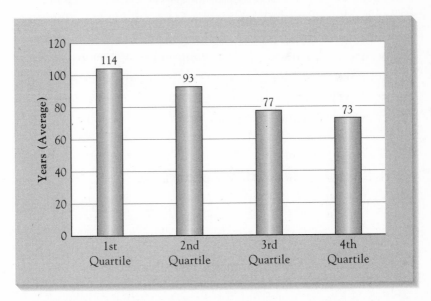

Note: The standard deviation of years in existence for the top quartile was 66 years; for quartile two, it was 72 years. The top quartile's smaller standard deviation validates the finding that top quartile companies have operated for a longer period of time than their closest peers.

on the art of competition will likely be, and what the imperative's impact on the company's financial performance could be.

- Next, they undertake an assessment to identify the imperative's attributes that are most meaningful to their business, as seen both through their and external observers' eyes. Based on this information, the next step is to evaluate their current performance relative to these attributes, set target performance levels, and create detailed plans to complete a portfolio of adjustments to achieve these goals.

- Finally, they execute their plans, measure their progress, and pursue continuous improvement based on brutally honest feedback.

These companies see sustainability as a means to growth and long-term success and have taken decisive action. Their successful approaches offer clear lessons for companies seeking to ensure their own sustainability over the long term. The combination of competitive advantages earned from their efforts to embrace sustainability and enhanced corporate agility make it more likely that these companies will continue to sustain their existence for longer periods of time than their peers.

What Sustainable Market Leaders Do

To create value today and into the future, Sustainable Market Leaders

- View sustainability as a means for value creation today and tomorrow and reject the view that sustainability is achieved through altruism and risk mitigation
- Challenge assumptions about market dynamics to identify and explore adjacent business opportunities

- Identify environmental and social problems to solve with available capabilities in a (mutually) beneficial way
- Employ sustainability as an additional lens to evaluate operational inefficiencies and a telescope through which to view distant but approaching growth opportunities
- Accept that embracing sustainability is prickly and hard, not warm and fuzzy; as a result, employ small, smart changes to what they already do to create value
- Go beyond employee engagement to employee co-creation (engagement is good, what companies do with the engagement is far more valuable)
- Develop networks of peers, non-peers, academics, and NGOs to find and evaluate ideas to build a pipeline of innovations and enhance corporate agility
- Continuously renew their sustainability strategy and management efforts

Conclusion

Sustainable Market Leaders inextricably link their sustainability management, corporate, and competitive strategy efforts to create value for stakeholders. They sharpen their value chain activities by integrating sustainability initiatives. And they engage with stakeholders to continuously renew their ability to create value into the future. As a result, Sustainable Market Leaders have become adept at managing two seemingly competitive demands: creating value today and tomorrow. Chapter Two sheds a critical light on how these companies are embracing sustainability as a means for competitive differentiation.

2

SUSTAINABLE MARKET LEADERS COMPETE ON SUSTAINABILITY

Chapter One defined "Sustainable Market Leaders" as companies that have integrated sustainability into their value chain activities today and their investments for tomorrow. This chapter reveals how Sustainable Market Leaders are creating value today and preparing to continue tomorrow. Sustainability has changed the terrain of competition. For example, buyers are now requiring suppliers to integrate sustainability as a condition to win and maintain business. The competitor that has integrated sustainability into their value chain activities is more likely to win this business. We will see this dynamic play out in the following story.

Monadnock: From ISO to Sustainable Market Leader

Incorporated in 1842, the town of Bennington, New Hampshire, is a well-balanced mix of nature, commerce, and the charm of days gone by. For as far as the eye can see, beautiful, mature trees serve as a serene background for the 1,400 residents who inhabit this town in houses bearing signs documenting construction in the mid-1800s.

Through the center of town runs the Contoocook River, 71 miles in length and emptying into the Merrimack River. The Contoocook is a source of local pride, high-quality materials, and renewable energy. Starting in 1819, the Butler family began to source flax from the banks of the Contoocook in order to produce handmade paper. In 1835, papermaking machinery was installed by the Bennington Paper Mills company near the Contoocook to produce paper for writing and blank books. After a local railroad was extended to reach Bennington, the paper company began to expand. The company now known as Monadnock Paper Mills (MPM) took its name in 1880 from the region's most prominent mountain: Mount Monadnock. Today MPM is viewed as one of the most innovative and sustainable paper companies in the United States.

A sense of community and a commitment to preserve the Contoocook River have enabled Monadnock to sustain itself for nearly two hundred years. These fundamental purposes are the reasons Monadnock was the first among its peers to install an environmental management system that complies with ISO 14001.[1]

It should be no surprise that Monadnock's early adoption of ISO 14001 has led it to be an exemplar of Sustainable Market Leaders that employ their sustainability efforts in order to differentiate themselves from their peers. For example, consider one of Monadnock's recent business wins. Gap Inc. sought a supplier of paper for their hang tags, the 2-inch-by-1-inch white paper tags that communicate an item's size, price, and SKU and that hang on the backs of sweaters, chambrays, and other apparel. As companies that seek competitive bids do, Gap cast a wide net to find the right supplier.

On a recent visit to the paper mill, I had the opportunity to meet with Richard Verney, MPM's chairman and chief executive officer, and Michelle Hamm, the company's manager of environmental services. After a tour of the historic facility, we had the chance to discuss how Monadnock earned Gap's business. According to Verney:

> Gap wanted to use more sustainable materials for their price tags. They visited our headquarters in Bennington, New Hampshire. An independent environmental consulting firm that they hired to verify our ISO 14001 documentation

accompanied them. Together Gap and the consulting firm held our feet to the fire to confirm that we do in fact do all of the things we say we do when it comes to environmental compliance. The result of that analysis was that yes, we do. We earned their business. Without our ISO 14001 documentation, we would not have their business today.

I also interviewed Jorge Perez-Olmo, who is the senior global marketing sourcing manager for Gap Brands. The manager responsible for overseeing the price tag decision, Jorge explained how Gap chose Monadnock over MPM's peers:

> We knew about Monadnock Paper. When we decided to source FSC [Forest Stewardship Council]-certified paper for our price tags, we reached out to Monadnock for more information. We visited their mill and we brought a third party with us to ask Monadnock Paper the technical questions about their ISO 14001 documentation. From a marketing standpoint, we wanted the right aesthetic and the right paper. We combined those with ISO 14001 compliance. If by any chance one of these three attributes was not aligned with the other two, we knew we would not pursue Monadnock's paper. At Monadnock, we got all the bases covered. Our social responsibility group and our third-party consulting firm both gave us the green light because they had all the documentation they needed. And from a marketing standpoint, the aesthetic and paper worked perfectly. So sourcing from Monadnock was an easy decision.

Connecting Sustainability with Corporate Strategy

In several of my interviews, I heard leaders make connections between the language of sustainability and the language of strategy. It is important that the two concerns share a common language. Practitioners at companies as diverse as Unilever, Centrica, and Cisco see the close association between sustainability and broader strategy. In fact, they used the same phrase to describe how their companies employ sustainability. These and other Sustainable Market Leaders called sustainability a "lens for evaluating and crafting the strategic direction" of their organizations.

Unilever is a Sustainable Market Leader. A main reason is the company's commitment to connecting sustainability with their corporate strategy. Following is a quote from Santiago Gowland, Unilever's vice president of brand and corporate responsibility at the time I interviewed him for *The Future of Value*.[2] I wholeheartedly recommend all companies follow this approach to thinking about how integrating sustainability can strengthen strategic decision making.

> The way I see sustainability and strategy is divided into four stages. The four stages are quite important to understand how Unilever has progressed on its sustainability journey.
>
> The first bucket is *compliance*. Compliance in a company has a lot to do with understanding environmental and social risks and regulations and then putting in place measurement and reporting systems. There is a broad range of guidelines and criteria to assess a company's impact, the Global Reporting Initiative for example. In this initial phase, a company will need to gain a deeper understanding of the social, economic, and environmental impact and then develop key performance indicators and begin to set targets and commitments to improve those impacts. So setting that agenda is the bedrock.
>
> The second stage is *integration*. Integration is where a company begins to understand the business potential of the sustainability agenda. Integration is all about fueling innovation, about finding new ways of doing things, ways that integrate the social, economic, and environmental impacts of the company's business. We developed a branding proposal that connects our corporate initiatives with how we engage

consumers in a deeper conversation about sustainability. That integration agenda has two main outputs for us. One is cost reduction because sustainability has a lot of low hanging fruit—less packaging, less energy, less water, et cetera. The other lever is equity enhancement in our brands. Having brands that are trusted by consumers becomes a differentiating element.

The third bucket is *transformation*. In this bucket corporate strategy as a whole is enhanced by the company's efforts to embrace sustainability. The interesting thing about transformation is that some companies reach a state where they redefine who they are and how they want to do business. They embed sustainability at the core of their corporate strategy, brand vision, company vision, and mission statements. In our last vision statement, Unilever demonstrated that we are progressing through this transformation step. We launched a new vision statement. The four pillars of our vision set out the long-term direction for the company—where we want to go and how we are going to get there:

- We work to create a better future every day.
- We help people feel good, look good, and get more out of life with brands and services that are good for them and good for others.
- We will inspire people to take small everyday actions that can add up to a big difference for the world.
- We will develop new ways of doing business with the aim of doubling the size of our company while reducing our environmental impact.

We also redeveloped our brand strategy position to capture the intention of becoming a force for good in society. We began to work on all of the enabling functions and processes to integrate this idea into everything that we do. From culture change and employee policies, to the way we engage with suppliers and partners to the priorities such as assigned to research and development. So everything in a way becomes part of this idea of sustainable development.

The fourth stage is *systemic change*. Systemic change requires finding new ways of doing business by working with others to accelerate social transformation. This is where we are focusing our efforts now.

Santiago shared a diagram (shown as Figure 2.1) that Unilever employs to identify "sweet spots" to pursue for growth. These sweet spots are found in the intersection of "core competencies and capabilities," "consumer concerns and expectations," "business growth strategy," and "social, economic, and environmental challenges."

Centrica, one of the United Kingdom's largest utilities and a perennial resident of the 100 Most Sustainable Companies ranking initiated by Corporate Knights, employs sustainability

Figure 2.1 How Unilever Has Integrated Sustainability into Its Process to Identify "Sweet Spots"

Lenses to look through

Core competencies and capabilities

Social, economic, and environmental challenges

"The sweet spot"

Consumer concerns and expectations (link to brands)

Business growth strategy

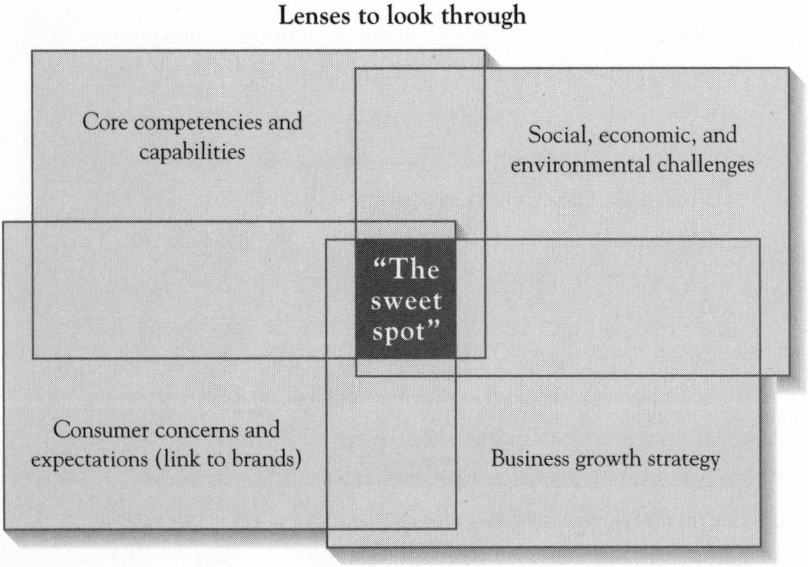

in a remarkably similar fashion. When asked to describe the role of sustainability at Centrica, Amelia Knott, the company's corporate responsibility manager, explained:

> Corporate responsibility (CR) is pretty much everything to do with how we do business. In early 2010, we launched a new CR strategy to map out the role of CR within our business and better integrate it with our stated business strategy. The CR strategy is built on our underlying values, behaviors, and the culture of the business. Next are the responsible business practices—areas such as supply chain and community engagement that we think all companies should be doing well. We then identified our focus areas, which are those aspects most integral to our business activities where we aim to play a leading role and where we have both challenges and opportunities due to the nature of our business, the number and type of people we employ, and the wider role we have to play in society.
>
> These focus areas, which inform both our long-term strategy and daily operations, include customers (which covers everything from customer service to vulnerable customers), people (how we look after our people, how we engage them, and the skills agenda as well), health and safety, and securing energy supplies. We're the largest energy supplier in the UK, and we have a responsibility to take care of long-term energy supplies for our domestic and business customers. So we must continually look to the future.
>
> The pinnacle of our strategy and what we think can differentiate us from others is a commitment to provide energy for a low-carbon world, together with everything that this entails—from skills to technology. But this is not just about CR, it's also completely woven into our corporate strategy, which makes it quite hard for us to separate out what are core business operations from what is "corporate responsibility" to both internal and external audiences. There are ways of looking at anything around our business through a CR lens.

Sustainability and Competitive Strategy: The Five Forces Model of Competition

As I mentioned in the Introduction to this book, sustainability's impact on the competitive landscape is best tested and viewed through the lens of Michael Porter's watershed Five Forces Model of Competition: suppliers, buyers, substitutes, new entrants, and industry rivalry (see Figure 2.2).[3] As the reader will discover, Sustainable Market Leaders are embracing sustainability not for altruistic purposes but for demonstrable, competitive differentiation. Their peers' decision to not adapt to sustainability's concerns and interests provides in itself another level of differentiation for Sustainable Market Leaders. Let's examine changes in each of the five forces.

Figure 2.2 Sustainability's Impact on Competitive Strategy Seen Through Michael Porter's Five Forces Model

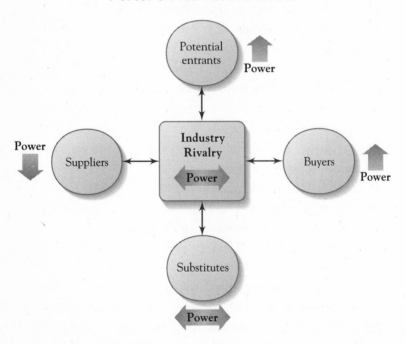

Note: Reprinted with permission.

Suppliers

When Sustainable Market Leaders commit to sustainability, they place many new demands on already overburdened suppliers. Procurement requirements range from demonstrating ISO 14001 compliance to maintaining decent worker practices in the suppliers' factories. For example, recently Dallas, Texas–based Travelocity accepted Hilton Worldwide hotels into the company's Green Hotel Directory, a story that is described further later in Chapter Seven. Alison Presley, manager of Travelocity's Travel for Good program, illustrated the real need for suppliers to demonstrate their sustainability commitments by describing how the company's program allows hotels to appear in the company's directory:

> The day the press release went out announcing our addition of Hilton Worldwide hotels into the Green Hotel Directory, a sustainability manager at a rival hotel chain called me. He said, "Wait, why can't we join the Green Hotel Directory?" And I said, "I would love to accept your program. However you don't have an external audit at this time. I would strongly encourage you to find an auditor and then show us the proof of the pudding. And if you do measure up, we would be happy to accept your program." So it has in fact raised awareness within the industry and certainly among the big hotel chains.

To bring their new compliance requirements to life, Sustainable Market Leaders require their suppliers to conduct and file self-assessment reports documenting their compliance with each sustainability article in the buyer's supplier code of conduct. Those suppliers whose actions are found lacking are subject to onsite factory audits. The upshot of these audits is the development and presentation to the supplier's management of a remediation plan. The managers have two choices upon receipt of the remediation plan: either take all recommended actions by a specified date or lose the buyer's business. In this way sustainability has weakened suppliers' power in many of their business relationships.

Buyers

To better understand their current state of power, we need to distinguish between institutional buyers and individual consumers.

If power in relationships between suppliers and buyers is a zero-sum game, then, in a business environment driven by sustainability, buyers capture power from suppliers and vice versa. The Monadnock Paper–Gap Inc. story provides a clear example of this new dynamic. Partly as a result of Gap's choosing Monadnock, several of Monadnock's peers are now also working to become ISO 14001 compliant.

Regarding power relationships between producers and individual consumers, the outcome is still unsettled. For more than a decade individual consumers have communicated, through primary research, their preference for products manufactured via environmentally and/or socially conscious methods. Yet these consumers have yet to vote, en masse, with their wallets. The most-often cited reason is the "premium price" placed on such goods relative to goods produced through "traditional" methods. Because it is so huge (consumer purchases account for two-thirds of U.S. gross domestic product) this category of buyers represents a dormant source of power and influence that, if wielded effectively, could force companies to make environmentally and socially conscious manufacturing methods the new "traditional" approach to value creation.

Substitutes

In the business-to-business market sustainable substitutes are gaining power. Monadnock's FSC-certified commercial printing paper is an example of a product that is earning new revenue for its organization. Monadnock Paper saw an opportunity in a very crowded market: the packaging paper business. They sensed that a high-quality, high-environmentally friendly paper product could lead to new sales in a new market for the company. As Richard Verney, Monadnock's chairman and CEO recounted:

> About a year and a half ago we entered the packaging paper business. A zillion people make packaging. We came out with the highest-content, post-consumer waste packaging products in the market. And that grabbed people's attention and generated sales. So it's pretty easy to see the benefits.
>
> Now of course once that happens, all of your competitors immediately say, "We've got to do that too." And so they hop on board and your competitive advantage, your differentiation, sometimes doesn't last that long because the paper business is very competitive. But I think there are as many examples as you want about the fact that having a sustainability profile is good for the volume of business you do and for the bottom line.
>
> If sustainability is something your customers want, you've got to figure out a way to do it that doesn't necessarily add to your cost because they're not going to pay for it. The early adopters, which I think we've been, do have an advantage. And part of that advantage is not just being first but by establishing your reputation early in the marketplace tends to stay with you, unless you really screw it up, and that's of value.

In the individual consumer market, there have been a few notable successes. The Toyota Prius was the first mass-produced hybrid (that is, it can run on either gas or electricity) vehicle when it was introduced in Japan in 1997. By September 2010 more than two million "Prii" (in February 2011 Toyota asked the public writ large to decide the plural term of Prius; *Prii* was the most popular choice) had been sold worldwide. But until consumers change their buying behavior by placing a greater emphasis on sustainability when making purchases, sustainably produced substitutes will struggle to gain market share.

Potential Entrants

In both the consumer and business customer markets, many new sustainability-conscious entrants are trying to capture market share. But the best measure of their success effect to date is not how much share they have captured but how many subsequent maneuvers incumbents have made in response to the new entrants' efforts. For example, consider the environmentally friendly household cleaner market niche. Startup Seventh Generation's progress eventually convinced Clorox to also enter this niche. To gain a foothold there, Clorox pioneered a game-changing (and perhaps unforeseeable) relationship with the Sierra Club. In return for the rights to print the Sierra Club logo on each unit of its GreenWorks products, Clorox agreed to pay a single-digit percentage of profits to the Sierra Club. In this way, nongovernmental organizations (NGOs) such as Sierra Club are gaining power in the manufacturer-consumer relationship.

Similarly, Tesla, the Silicon Valley electric vehicle startup, has affected the automotive industry without gaining even 1 percent of the market. Their mere presence, and the celebrity-like attention their founder has received, have led car manufacturers such as Nissan (Leaf) and GM (Volt) to allocate billions of dollars to their own electric vehicle development efforts.

Industry Rivalry: "Co-opetition" and Competitive Differentiation

The industry rivalry force in Porter's Five Forces model refers to competition among companies in a given industry. As I mentioned earlier, I believe Sustainable Market Leaders' pursuit of sustainability ahead of their peers has changed the terrain of competition. Fifteen years ago Barry Nalebuff and Adam Brandenburger coined the term *co-opetition* to describe "a revolutionary mind-set that combines competition and cooperation."[4] They encouraged companies to view competition through the lens of game theory: a 50 percent of a $1 billion pie is better than a 90 percent of a $400 million pie. Their message was clear: look beyond the traditional boundaries of competition for growth opportunities and risk mitigation tactics. I believe that industry rivalry has morphed into a curious state of uneven co-opetition.

Their struggle to find common ground mirrors the struggles many private sector competitors are facing in their efforts to address sustainability. More and more progressive companies are finding that collaborating with strange bedfellows, including their competitors, is good for all involved. Here's how these companies are engaging in co-opetition.

HP, Dell, and Lenovo remain fierce competitors in multiple markets. Yet they've put their competitive instincts aside to develop, alongside other competitors, a standard—known as the Electronic Industry Citizenship Coalition (EICC)—set of sustainable manufacturing expectations for their common suppliers. Numerous other industries are following suit, including the financial services, chemicals, and automotive industries. These traditional competitors, enlightened by a collectively shared understanding that their self-interests over the long term are inextricably linked with the common interest, are collaborating to bring about adoption of sustainability ideals and aspirations among as large a critical mass of businesses as possible.

Gap Brand's Perez-Olmo described how Gap collaborates with competitors for the common good:

> Word of our commitment and progress toward becoming sustainable has reached other retailers. Our social responsibility colleagues receive calls from other retailers that are organizing summits where brand retailers share best practices. My social

responsibility colleagues come out of these summits and say, "So and so from this company is going to call you because they want to find out how this happened." And we share best practices. Because we believe sharing best practices can promote sustainable ideals and performance.

Let's turn now to competitive differentiation, the flipside of co-opetition between industry rivals. After all, Sustainable Market Leaders are pursuing global sustainability to ensure their own sustainability, not to merely serve more altruistic purposes. When I asked each company interviewed for this book to describe sustainability's role within their organizations, more than 90 percent responded with a variant of "Sustainability is core to our competitive strategies." Implicitly, these companies believe that leading their peers in adopting and committing to sustainability will help them capture market share.

In this way, Sustainable Market Leaders face a paradox. Adopting sustainability ahead of their peers improves their defense of their share of market. Yet the more suppliers that adopt sustainable practices and the more industry standards are created that help these Sustainable Market Leaders and their peers communicate their sustainability-oriented advantages relative to their competitors' efforts, the easier it is to ensure the Sustainable Market Leader's long-term success. Thus, industry rivalry has become both more complicated and more intense due to sustainability.

The state of simultaneous competition and collaboration is perhaps best summarized by Tim Mohin, Advanced Micro Devices' director of corporate responsibility:

Companies definitely are competing on a differentiation basis. There's always this line to walk when we collaborate versus compete. In some cases it makes sense for competitors to collaborate on issues of social good and I'd use the conflict metals case as an example. We're dealing now with this very

important issue that's become law. We are much stronger
working together. At the same time, you can see some
companies trying to sort of gather more attention upon
themselves for the good works. And so there's always a little bit
of tension in those collaborative relationships. But clearly that
works in some cases. In other cases we are competing against
one another for recognition in terms of lists.

Sustainable Market Leaders are beginning to design competitive differentiation strategies based on their progress on and insights from their sustainability efforts. These companies are doing so in order to capture and retain customers and design market entry strategies, among other performance-enhancing reasons. While Chapter Three dives deeper into the connection among sustainability, strategy, and financial performance, I conclude this chapter with a look at how Sustainable Market Leaders are translating their sustainability efforts into differentiation.

Sustainability as Vehicle to Capture Customers

Earlier I discussed Travelocity and its Travel for Good program. Now I look back at how that program got started. Doing so will help us better understand how sustainability can serve as a vehicle to capture customers.

Travelocity competes in an industry where competitive differentiation is, at best, fleeting. The online travel agency (OTA) market sells a commoditized product, customers do not incur costs to switch among providers, and asymmetric pricing tactics are quickly matched. As Alison Presley explained:

I would say probably 99 percent of the time our prices are exactly
the same as our competitors. So our question has always been,
"How do we make people care about choosing our service?"

Travelocity believes that, all other things equal, pockets of consumers value a hotel destination's environmental sustainability attributes enough to choose so-called green hotels over hotels that have not earned this distinction. The company has introduced its Travel for Good service in order to attract these consumers away from other OTAs. Presley commented:

> We want to be seen as a socially responsible company. I think an important factor in that part of our brand is the sustainable travel piece. So in 2006 a group of really engaged employees approached upper management with this idea: "We want to make sure that what we do has meaning and that the negative impacts of travel are reduced and the positive impacts are enhanced." The executive team loved the idea and they formalized what they wanted the program to be. They named the program Travel for Good. Our mission is "Making the world a better place one trip at a time."
>
> We launched a program with just 200 hotels. Today I'm proud to say that we have over 2,500 and growing. We're hoping to have 3,000 by the end of this year. While I have a separate green travel micro site, I felt flagging these "green hotels" site-wide was vital to attract even the lightest green shopper. That is the type of consumer who buys organic cereal but is not hard core about organics. In other words, the consumer who is open to green, but is not going to pay more.
>
> So we've been really proud of that, and what has happened is that in Q1 of 2010 green hotel bookings were 65 percent higher than non-green hotel bookings. And a lot of people were really surprised to see that, but in a way I wasn't because I already knew that these were some of our most engaged hotel partners. These are the ones out there thinking really hard about the customer experience for all levels. And another thing we learned is that this program is good for our bottom line.

Finally, green hotels also get better customer reviews.
And that translates. Whether you're noticing it as green or
just noticing as just a great hotel, customers prefer them. We're
in a very commoditized space and we know that our prices
are consistent with our competitors. So how do we convince
customers that we're the ones they want to spend their
money with, right? We equip customers to find green hotel
choices.

Sustainability as Market Entry Strategy

In 1835, under Royal Charter, the Bank of Australasia was established. Over the years, the bank merged with other firms, eventually becoming known as ANZ Bank. In 1970 ANZ Bank merged
with English, Scottish, and Australian Bank to form Australia &
New Zealand Banking Group Limited. The 175-year-old company
knows a thing or two about sustaining itself over the long term.
So it comes as no surprise that Australia & New Zealand Bank
has made sustainability (the bank uses the phrase "corporate
responsibility" or CR to refer to the ethos of sustainability) an
integral part of its business strategy to become a super-regional
bank. According to Julie Bisinella, ANZ's head of corporate
responsibility:

> The benefits we see as a result of our efforts to integrate
> sustainability into daily business operations and corporate
> vision include attracting and retaining employees, This is
> particularly so in many countries in Asia. People in the region
> are interested in sustainability issues and want to contribute to
> meaningful solutions. This may be because they are much closer
> to some of the economic, social, and environmental issues and
> opportunities that people in developed countries may not feel
> as acutely.

One pillar of ANZ's market entry strategy is a planned reliance on local talent. As Bisinella explained:

> Our CEO has stated that we cannot have a growth strategy in Asia that relies exclusively on expatriates. We need to be able to attract and retain insiders with connections and an understanding of local markets, local businesses, and local issues and opportunities.

Bisinella concluded by noting that one benefit of prioritizing CR is the increased likelihood that the bank will be able to attract the talent it needs to achieve its super-regional bank vision:

> Being able to attract those "local insiders" means having a value proposition that encourages them to join ANZ. Given we are not currently the biggest banking brand in the region, the opportunity to be part of our growth story together with our commitment to responsible banking, is certainly helping with that.

Conclusion

Integration of sustainability by some but not all companies is altering the terrain of competition. Sustainable Market Leaders are finding ways to connect their sustainability efforts with ways to attract customers and enter new markets—two ways to create business value. Until all companies embrace sustainability, thus blunting the competitive edge earned by Sustainable Market Leaders, sustainability will continue to lead to commercial advantage. The next chapter sheds more light on how.

DIAGNOSTIC

The following questions will help you identify ways sustainability has altered your competitive reality by reviewing each of Porter's Five Forces of Competition.

Suppliers

1. Are the businesses to which you sell asking for information about your sustainability commitments, progress, and activities?
2. Do you know what percentage of each of these businesses' decisions are based on your answers to these sustainability questions?
3. Are you employing the collective set of these businesses' sustainability questions to evaluate and improve your commitments, progress, and activities?

Buyers

1. Has your company altered its procurement policies and processes to embrace ethical sourcing?
2. What specific adjustments have been made to do so?
3. Have you validated your questions with a stakeholder partner to confirm the questions you are asking of vendors will enable you to meet your sustainability goals?

Substitutes

1. Is the gestalt of sustainability on your target consumers' radar screens?
2. Do you compete in commodity markets where competitors that are further along on their sustainability journeys can claim market share from your products?
3. Have you tested whether your consumers would be more likely to purchase your products if you accelerated your efforts to embrace sustainability?

Potential New Entrants

1. Are your markets at risk of a disruptive technology that relies on a significantly lower amount of resource consumption?
2. Are your markets protected by high barriers to entry?
3. Can you employ your resources to scale down existing products or otherwise innovate to enter new markets?

Industry Rivalry

1. Are you collaborating more often with your primary competition?
2. Can you clearly and succinctly articulate the boundaries of information you are willing to share with peers in the guise of "serving the common interest"?
3. Would your front-line employees cite the same boundaries?

3

COMPETING ON SUSTAINABILITY CREATES VALUE

Chapter Two revealed how Sustainable Market Leaders' integration of sustainability has changed the terrain of competition. This chapter reveals several tactics Sustainable Market Leaders use as a means to create value for their stakeholders.

Three Reasons to "Wing It"

Imagine I came to you with the following business proposition. I want you to invest less than $10 million dollars to bring basic mobile phone banking services to a country of 15 million residents, only a fraction of whom currently hold bank accounts. As I describe the proposition, I note that 60 percent of your potential customers live on less than $3 per day. Would you invest in my proposal? Well if you were Australia & New Zealand Banking Group (ANZ Banking Group), the answer would be yes.

Fueled by a desire to earn a foothold in Asia and supported by a will to stay the course over the long term, ANZ launched Wing, a mobile banking solution in Cambodia in 2009. The Wing model is based on charging a nominal fee for every transaction over the Wing network. Transactions include cash withdrawals, person-to-person payments, and mobile phone fee payments. Account holding fees are not assessed, and no minimum account balances are required.

Wing has seen steady growth in adoption rates. One year after its launch, WING had over 100,000 registered customers.

Revenue is above predicted levels, with breakeven projected to occur in 2011.

While impressive in its own right, the real value Wing provides to ANZ Banking Group comes in three forms:

1. The product is achieving significant economic and social outcomes in Cambodia and for the group, particularly in financial inclusion, a key issue for governments in the region and a materiality issue for ANZ Banking Group. After all, 56 percent of Wing customers were previously unbanked; 67 percent of these customers are women.

2. Wing is providing ANZ with critical experience in mobile payments, the fastest-growing channel in financial services globally. In fact, McKinsey forecast the mobile money industry to be worth $7.5 billion by 2012. Mobile money has only been in existence for five or six years, and the Wing product enables ANZ to learn lessons that will enable the company to develop a broader mobile phone banking strategy for its business.

3. Wing provides ANZ with the ability to achieve significant corporate responsibility outcomes. The product has enabled over 2,000 Cambodians to gain income streams, training, and experience serving as Wing sales agents. Wing has introduced 60,000 people to the financial services industry in Cambodia, increasing by 10,000–12,000 every month in its first year of operation. And Wing serves as a tangible example to key stakeholders of how ANZ can make a focused contribution to economic and social development goals (both rural and urban) in Asia Pacific countries.

Compare the reasons behind Wing's success with the challenges faced by Ellen, a real but pseudonymous environmental, health, and safety executive who is tirelessly working to embrace sustainability. Ellen has worked at her company, a commercial property management company, for twenty-two years. She is convinced that sustainability is not a passing fad, but a set of challenges her company needs to embrace to succeed long term.

Between March and November 2010, Ellen has built a sustainability council, consisting of representatives from every department and business unit. Attendance at the council's meetings has been promising; only at two of the five meetings (the council meets every other month) did one or more members fail to attend. Ellen's aspiration for the council is for it to serve as a vehicle to integrate sustainability into her company's core strategies. But here she has run into significant organizational resistance. Despite recognition as a leading performer among her peers, Ellen has been unable to gain sign-off on the three stewardship ideas for which she's sought investment in and approval of from her senior management team. A little digging revealed that senior management does not view sustainability as concomitant with business performance, since their customers have yet to demand solutions manufactured with stewardship top of mind.

The key learning? Ellen's failure was due to her inability to present sustainability in terms that were meaningful to senior leadership. The initial spark behind a company's interest in sustainability (for example, do the right thing) runs the risk of running out of fuel if the business fails to grasp the business case to embrace sustainability. Whereas personal conviction can adequately serve as the initial spark behind a company's interest in sustainability, a powerful business case must serve as the eternal flame to nurture an organization's pursuit of sustainability.

Translating Advantage into Performance

In his book, *Profit from the Core*, Chris Zook defines "adjacent business opportunities" as a company's continual moves into related segments or businesses that utilize and, usually, reinforce the strength of the profitable core.[1] Sustainable Market Leaders intrinsically believe that embracing sustainability will create more value for shareholders and other stakeholders. To convert their sustainability-led competitive strategy advantages into actual earnings drivers of enhanced financial performance, these companies are identifying adjacent business opportunities to pursue new revenue on the basis of their sustainability efforts.

Here are some ways in which Sustainable Market Leaders identify sustainability-led adjacent business opportunities:

- Test the alignment between current products and services and issues of simultaneous importance to the company and its stakeholders (what we call "issues of materiality")
- Apply sustainability lens to reevaluate customer concerns
- Ask "Why?" and "Why not?" questions through the lens of sustainability

Test Alignment Between Current Products and Services and Issues of Materiality

As we'll see in greater detail in Chapter Four, Sustainable Market Leaders conduct materiality assessments to better identify and prioritize the sustainability issues that are most meaningful to both their company and their stakeholders. After conducting their materiality assessment, ANZ Banking Group identified five corporate responsibility priorities:

1. Employ responsible business practices.
2. Provide and support education and employment opportunities.
3. Improve customers' financial capabilities.
4. Use its resources and skills as a bank to bridge urban and rural divides.
5. Promote urban sustainability.

The company then mapped its primary go-to-market programs, what they refer to as "flagship programs," to assess alignment between their products and services and their corporate
responsibility priorities. (See Figure 3.1 for a matrix of CR priorities and flagship programs.)

ANZ Banking Group's corporate responsibility priorities list
is, in effect, the components of the company's sustainability lens.
That lens clarifies how ANZ's corporate responsibility (the
company refers to sustainability as "corporate responsibility")
connects to its value creation efforts. Initiatives (such as Wing)
to improve financial inclusion in the bank's Asia Pacific division
demonstrate ANZ's commitment to employ responsible practices, promote education and employment, enhance financial
capability, and bridge the urban and rural divides (by enabling
money transfers between persons employed in the city to persons
residing in rural areas).

The activity illustrated in Figure 3.1 can be quite powerful.
In one diagram, a company can "map" its products and services
with its materiality issues. One can imagine creating a similar
matrix and mapping current offerings down the left side. The
columns without any shading could represent opportunities to
pursue. Intersections without matches may represent growth
opportunities, risks for value destruction, or both.

Reevaluate Customer Concerns from the Perspective of Sustainability

United Parcel Services (UPS) has been working to integrate
sustainability into their strategies, processes, and culture for ten
years. Not content to rest on its progress with integrating sustainability internally, UPS is now making its sustainability expertise
available to its customers. For example, as Lynnette McIntire,
director of corporate reputation management, shared:

Figure 3.1 Matrix of ANZ Banking Group's Corporate Responsibility Priorities and Flagship Programs

Region	Flagship Programs 2010–2011	Corporate Responsibility Priorities					
		Responsible Practices	Education and Employment	Financial Capability	Bridging Urban and Rural Divides	Urban Sustainability
Global	Community Invesment Fund					
	Volunteering/AVI					
	Disaster Relief and Recovery					
Australia	Saver Plus					
	Money/Minded					
	Progress Loans					
	Money Business					
	Reconciliation Action Plan					
	Disability Action Plan					
	Given the Chance					
APE&A	Wing					
	Banking the Unbanked					
	Rural Bank in China					
New Zealand	Saver Plus					
	Money/Minded					
	Maori Financial Knowledge					

Source: ANZ Banking Group

Sustainability has led us to look at incremental innovation, which we've always done internally but not necessarily from a product perspective. As an example, we've always had a packaging and design lab. Let's say we have a customer and we have huge damage claims from them all the time. Through this lab we look at the customer's packaging systems and their products and try to figure out how to minimize those damages.

Now with sustainability there's a whole new layer to that about, "Well, what are the materials that you're using? What are the environmental components of that packaging?" And damages itself is a green issue. If you're trying to minimize your environmental footprint and products are broken in transport, then you have to manufacture and ship out a replacement product. It essentially doubles your footprint. So now we're talking to customers from that perspective as well. We've introduced a customer program called, "eco responsible packaging," which uses the package lab's expertise, from a green perspective, on a contractual, fee-based arrangement.

I say more about UPS's sustainability efforts in Chapter Four.

ASK "Why" and "Why Not" Sustainability Questions

It's an understatement to say that as of late 2010 Advanced Micro Devices (AMD) has changed radically. Simply put, the company has spun off its manufacturing capabilities into a joint venture and rebranded to place a greater emphasis on its chip designs. The rebranding has necessitated the creation and adoption of a new strategy for the company. Tim Mohin has been actively involved in AMD's new strategy creation efforts:

Recently a group of us talked about our new Fusion line of products which are pretty innovative. Essentially from a layman's point of view, Fusion puts a graphics processing unit and a central processing unit together on the same piece of silicon. Doing so not only enables power savings, but it also just opens up all kinds of performance capabilities. It's essentially like having a supercomputer in your notebook.

We asked ourselves, "Why is AMD Fusion a big deal from a social or environmental context?" We started going down the list of things that people can do using this equipment that could help society in some way, shape, or form. And so right now I'm kicking off a project to look at case studies, to research looking along the lines of environmental stewardship for the modeling applications for example that would be leveraged through this technology.

I'm also looking down the medical research line, looking down a couple of other lines and gathering those case studies to develop where is that technology enabling social good in society. There are two ideas there. One is energy efficiency. The more we make our products energy efficient, the better they sell, and obviously the better it is for the environment. The second idea is enabling social causes or improvements through our technology. Again, it helps us sell our products but it also does social good.

If you go from where we are today to where we're going to be at the end of this year with the Fusion, if you look for like performance, we're going from potentially four chips down to two chips. So what really are these products being used for? What could they be used for? If we look at society as a series of problems to solve, how can our core competencies address those problems? You start thinking about new possibilities like, "If we are able to inspire and motivate scientists in the supercomputer range to use our technology, that's great for business, it's great for them, and their research should benefit society."

As we saw earlier in the chapter, Sustainable Market Leaders employ sustainability as a way to strengthen their competitive strategies, thus improving their ability to create business value.

These efforts are leading to financial performance enhancements that can be seen through an evaluation of the traditional drivers of the income statement: revenue and expenses.

Increasing Revenue

Sustainable Market Leaders leave no stones unturned in their quest to drive revenue growth responsibly. Following are examples of how these companies are both charging a premium for products that enhance their customers' sustainability performance and adjusting products to better satisfy social or environmental needs.

Charge a Premium Price

Sustainable Market Leaders are more and more frequently able to both charge and receive a premium price for their less environmentally harmful products by clearly communicating the energy savings and thus cost savings that their green products can deliver for customers. But is this business case widely accepted and valued by institutions and individuals? Let's briefly look at each segment's willingness to pay a premium price.

The business-to-business market is showing greater interest in vendors' sustainability efforts when evaluating vendor proposals. Procurement officers are asking vendors savvy environmental questions. Indications suggest vendors' answers to these environmental questions can influence buyers' vendor-of-choice decisions. Consider the enterprise market for laptops. Institutions replace their information technology every three years. If a technology company can prove its energy saving technology will earn companies a positive return on investment before the three-year cycle starts anew, then the company is likely to receive a premium price. Companies are receiving a slight price premium for laptops that can demonstrate that they reduce customers' energy consumption per laptop over the life of the laptop.

The individual consumer is less willing to pay more for products that will save them money over the products' useful life. Many surveys have assessed individual consumers' green buying behavior. Many find consumers very willing to buy green products, but they also find that consumers are not buying more green products as a percentage of their total product purchases. Let's consider the findings from a recent study by the Grocery Manufacturers Association and Deloitte. The survey found that 95 percent of shoppers surveyed are open to considering green products, 67 percent actively look for green products, only 47 percent find them, and just 22 percent purchase something green on their shopping trips. What is the disconnect between consumer interest in and actual purchase of green products? The report reveals that "shoppers don't understand why a green product should cost more if it was manufactured with less packaging or it was transported less distance."[2]

Herein lies the foundation for a successful business case to charge institutions (and receive) a premium price for green products. Manufacturers need to consistently deliver and communicate that their products save consumers money over substitute products to (prospective) buyers to successfully charge a premium for such added benefits (or, seen another way, reduced costs). Similarly, buyers must be willing and able to value the benefits of green products.

Increase Volume Sold

Another way to assess sustainability's ability to drive revenue growth is through the lens of quantity of solutions sold. Sustainable Market Leaders are employing four tactics to increase their sustainability-oriented solutions sales volume (see Figure 3.2):

1. New solutions to existing customers
2. New solutions to new customers

Figure 3.2 Sustainability Growth Tactics

		Existing	New
Target Customers	New	Emphasize sustainability commitment and solution's sustainability profile	Emphasize your brand and unique sustainability story
	Existing	Emphasize sustainability commitment and solution's sustainability profile	Emphasize link between deep understanding of customer's needs and your competencies

Solutions

3. Existing solutions to existing customers

4. Existing solutions to new customers

The next section of the chapter highlights the new solutions (lower right-hand) quadrant of Figure 3.2. The existing solutions quadrant isn't covered in depth here; from experience, value from traditional solutions is most effectively unlocked by smartly emphasizing the additive sustainability advantages these solutions have over competitors' solutions.

New Solutions to Existing Customers. Sustainable Market Leaders are actively seeking opportunities to enable their enterprise customers to lower their Scope 1, 2, and 3 greenhouse gas emissions, as defined by the Greenhouse Gas Protocol Initiative.[3] As discussed elsewhere in the book, stakeholders are actively (and visibly) holding organizations accountable for their greenhouse gas (GHG) footprints in both actual and relative terms.

As a service provider to many of the world's largest organizations, UPS regularly receives requests about the levels of carbon emissions associated with its offerings. As McIntyre explained, listening to customers has led to the creation of a new product:

> The product is called "UPS Carbon Neutral." We started calculating customers' carbon emissions associated with their shipments, at the request of the customers. In particular, a lot of European customers requested this information. And since we were already calculating our own carbon emissions, Scope 1, 2, and 3 (by the way which our competitors do not all do), we knew we could calculate this information for our customers. In the process of offering them that information, their next natural question was, "Oh, and can you offset the carbon emissions associated with our shipments?" To which we said, "We'll figure that out."
>
> Now offsetting frankly was not our primary modus operandi for mitigating our carbon impact. We wanted to do it inside the company and I think that's the responsible way to do it. But our customers asked us to look at this so that's what we did. Now a normal new product in UPS can take anywhere from eighteen to twenty-four months. Because our customers were asking us about this, because we saw it as an opportunity, because we had a bunch of people who championed it, because the management committee saw it as an opportunity, because we were hearing from our regional partners in Europe that this was something that we needed to do and that a competitor was already offering it, we said, "We've got to speed this up." So we actually went from concept to commercial solution in less than nine months!

New Solutions to New Customers. Marks & Spencer (M&S) is the United Kingdom's fifth-largest retailer, according to the January 2010 report, *The UK Top 20 Retailers*, developed by World Market Intelligence.[4] By all accounts significant growth in the UK retail market (or almost any retail market worldwide) is at best difficult to achieve. The market, dominated by Tesco, counts several other long-established companies with strong local household names, such as Sainsbury, Morrisons, and Kingfisher.

Driven by a desire to grow responsibly, in 2007 M&S launched Plan A, a collection of one hundred sustainability-oriented commitments to be achieved within five years. During the next three years, Plan A has provided a positive return on the company's investment, including enhanced brand reputation. Emboldened by their success to date in activities such as increasing reliance on renewable energy, M&S sensed a market opportunity in the utilities industry. Trading on their enhanced brand reputation as a responsible retailer, the company forged a partnership with Scottish and Southern Energy to launch M&S Energy to supply households with electricity and gas. For every unit of energy M&S Energy customers use, an equal unit of clean energy is generated and put back onto the United Kingdom's energy grid. To date, M&S Energy has signed up more than 350,000 customers and expanded its product offerings to include solar energy products.

In the process M&S has found ways to leverage M&S Energy to strengthen retail customers' ties to the retailer. Specifically, M&S Energy customers are incentivized to use less energy, in return receiving discount vouchers useable in M&S stores throughout the country.

Reducing Expenses

When companies first tackle sustainability, most are more successful at reducing expenses than at raising revenues. There are at least two reasons for this.

First, cost savings are more often, but not always, directly under a company's control. Want to save costs and reduce carbon emissions? Simple—employ boats instead of air freight to transport your products. Not hard to find a shipping company willing to take on new business. Want to increase revenue and reduce carbon emissions? You will likely need to convince someone to buy something they either haven't previously bought or haven't previously bought from you.

Second, many sustainability managers are more focused on the worthwhile cause of risk mitigation than the equally worthwhile pursuit of opportunities. As a group, sustainability managers were environmental health and safety (EH&S) professionals before taking the mantle as sustainability manager. EH&S professionals are responsible for ensuring safety and compliance within a company's owned operations; efficiency, not opportunity, is their primary language.

To be clear, connecting sustainability initiatives with cost reduction goals and results is a powerful lever to create value that both your shareholders and stakeholders will respect. Sustainable Market Leaders excel at recognizing and embracing systemic inefficiencies that simultaneously embrace sustainability and reduce costs. Mounting evidence suggests that five core expense areas are the most ripe for cost take-outs: carbon emissions, energy consumption, logistics, materials, and labor.[5]

Carbon Emissions

Carbon is the first new and widespread expense category added to the income statements of companies in the twenty-first century. The Kyoto Protocol, enacted in 1997, planted the seeds for carbon trading markets in developed countries. The European Union (EU) sprouted the world's first carbon market, the European Union's Emission Trading Scheme (EU ETS). Country participants set annual limits for plants located in their country and then distribute permits in the same amounts. Plants that emit more carbon than their allowances must compensate the host countries through permits acquired on the open market. The structure of the market puts in place two economic benefits for companies that emit less than their allowances. First, these plants can (and do) sell their unused permits through the EU ETS to plants needing additional allowances. Second, these plants hold the line on current expenses relative to their competition.

How expensive are carbon emissions? According to research conducted by Trucost, if carbon costs $28.24 per metric ton of emissions in 2012, total carbon costs would represent more than 1 percent of corporate revenue. The sector facing the biggest financial risk is utilities, which emits nearly 60 percent of all operation greenhouse gases from the S&P 500. If the thirty-four utilities in the S&P 500 had to pay for their emissions, their earnings would slide 45 percent. But in looking at risks to individual companies, the financial implications vary widely, from causing earnings to fall anywhere from less than 1 percent to 117 percent. For 203 companies, carbon costs would amount to less than 1 percent, and 71 companies' earnings would fall 10 percent or more.[6]

Sustainable Market Leaders view carbon reduction efforts as necessities today, regardless of whether the market has set a price for carbon.

Energy Consumption

As industry has grown, so has its energy consumption. Before we reached a $150 per oil barrel price point, companies were more hesitant to consider alternative energy sources. Then growth became expensive. Companies began to consider alternatives; the investment community continued to demand growing levels of net income and free cash flow. In response, some companies dabbled; a bank of solar panels here, a block purchase of renewable energy credits there. Intent signaled . . . a good start made.

Sustainable Market Leaders question the assumption that growth automatically requires greater energy consumption. They seek holes in the equation; alternative approaches to achieve their desired outcome: to grow while consuming less energy. After all, energy is an expense; finding ways to uncouple the growth = increased demand for energy assumption opens up new opportunities. And if one word described how Sustainable Market Leaders view sustainability, it is *opportunity*.

Logistics

The sustainability movement, much like the quality movement before it, is leading companies to reexamine their mature processes. The act of moving a product from point A to point B has gone through several revolutions. Horse and buggy gave way to railroads; national development of highways gave birth to trucking; airplanes enabled companies to access the lower costs of employing offshore labor.

Each new transportation method led to greater time and expense efficiencies. Want your products to reach your customers faster? Choose air freight instead of shipping. But the underbelly of these new technologies became obvious to the investment community when a price for carbon began to be established.

Sustainable Market Leaders apply innovative thinking to grow revenue while reducing logistics costs. Massive Wal-Mart is employing similar thinking. A company executive recently revealed the giant retailer has found a way to save $3.5 million in transportation expenses annually just by reducing the size of toy packaging imported from Asia. Doing so resulted in 727 fewer shipments of ocean containers. The standard shipping rates for those containers from Asia can be well over $1,000, so the savings for the company are significant.[7]

Wal-Mart is one company that has garnered cost and environmental savings from logistical adjustments. For example, by installing auxiliary power units Wal-Mart has been able to save $26 million annually in fuel costs for its fleet of 7,200 trucks. The power units enable the drivers to keep the truck cabs' temperature regulated during mandatory ten-hour breaks from the road. This eliminates the waste from letting the truck engine idle for ten hours.[8]

AT&T sees future value in investing heavily now to replaces its current fleet of vehicles with alternative fuel vehicles. Early in 2010 AT&T launched a $560 million initiative to deploy more than 15,000 alternative fuel vehicles over the next ten years. Randall Stephenson, AT&T's CEO, described the investment this way: "Economic times are tough, but tough times make it even more important to look for efficient solutions. This is part of a long-term strategy that will help us continue to cut operating costs, reduce emissions in the communities we serve and make our business even more sustainable."[9]

As carbon emission becomes priced more pervasively, companies are likely to consider whether sourcing domestically (thus further reducing the carbon footprint of moving products from overseas) makes economic sense. At least one Sustainable Market Leader is analyzing this scenario. While factoring in the price of carbon emissions alone does not dramatically alter the economics of overseas sourcing, material, labor, supplier auditing, and transportation costs are conspiring to make the overseas versus domestic sourcing debate less one-sided.

Materials and Components

Since 2000, demand for virgin materials has skyrocketed as affluence levels have risen, especially in developing countries. As quickly as demand drove prices up, Wall Street imploded, credit markets froze, discretionary income plunged, causing supply of virgin materials to outpace demand. Prices deflated.

Such volatility challenges even the best-laid plans. Sustainable Market Leaders are reducing their exposure to future volatility in the commodities markets, not by entering long-term contracts at today's prices but by thinking in terms of sustainability. Two assumptions support this line of thought:

1. Reusing materials is more environmentally friendly than sourcing virgin materials.

2. The cost per unit of material of recycled materials is less than virgin materials.

So Sustainable Market Leaders are using more recycled material in their manufacturing processes. Some are also setting up intra-industry recycling systems or offering customers gift cards in return for their used products.

Wal-Mart reduces packaging and thereby increases profitability for both itself and its suppliers. Since 2008, the world's largest retailer has been working with suppliers to reduce packaging materials by 5 percent. According to Wal-Mart's calculations, the initiative will prevent millions of pounds of trash from reaching landfills and is projected to save 667,000 metric tons of carbon dioxide from entering the atmosphere. This is equal to taking 213,000 trucks off the road annually and saving 323,800 tons of coal and 66.7 million gallons of diesel fuel from consumption. This initiative will also save Wal-Mart and its suppliers about $11 billion. Wal-Mart alone can save up to $3.4 billion.[10]

As can be seen by the Wal-Mart story, Sustainable Market Leaders are reevaluating all value chain activities through the lens of sustainability to identify opportunities for financial and performance improvement. Consider Cisco. Cisco's decision to embrace sustainability led Edna Conway, who at the time of this book's completion directed sustainability initiatives for Cisco's Customer Value Chain Management organization, to integrate the value chain and sustainability lenses she applies to assess the efficacy of the organization's sustainability activities. First she developed the organization's strategy to focus on 4 Pillars of Sustainability: Labor Rights & Diversity; Human Health & Safety; Effective Use & Preservation of Natural Resources; and Product Security & Integrity. Edna explained:

We have made sustainability one of our value chain business filters. Key to doing so is integrating the sustainability filter with all others through which we measure a world-class value chain. To do that we require that a successful sustainable activity not only positively address one of Cisco's 4 Pillars of value chain sustainability but also positively impact one or more of three world-class value chain filters: One is quality. Two is cost. The third filter is process efficiency.

An essential component of Cisco's solutions is printed circuit board assemblies (think motherboards for computers). The sustainability filter spurred an analysis of the amount of water used in the manufacture of these printed circuit board assemblies. Edna shared a recent story about how integrating the sustainability filter with key world-class value chain filters helped Cisco save about $2 million annually, reduced energy consumption and water usage, and streamlined the board assembly process by eliminating the water wash step:

> We migrated our manufacturers to a "no-wash manufacturing process." That means that water is no longer used to clean any debris remaining on the PCBAs [printed circuit board assemblies] after soldering. Large, complex PCBAs were washed for quality and aesthetic reasons. Collaborating with our manufacturing partners to convert to newer and different types of solder chemistry, we could eliminate virtually all PCBA residue. By applying the new solder chemistries across the board, we were able to conserve 20 million gallons of water. Applying our mandate that a sustainability activity was not a value chain "win" until other filters had been positively impacted, our analysis showed that
>
> • Eliminating the water also eliminated the need for power to the washing tools. We saved 12 million kWh annually.

- 12 million kWh reduction equated with 8,600 metric tons of GHG emissions that were eliminated.

- By switching to the alternative solder chemistries, we also saw an increase in the quality of the PCBAs.

- We were able to eliminate a step in the fab process.

Overall, we saved water, energy reduced GHG emissions, improved quality, made our process more efficient, and saved about $2 million annually with this initiative.

Labor

At first glance, cost savings and a vibrant workforce might look a mismatch in terms. Think about the terms *labor* and *cost savings* in the same sentence. What comes to mind? Shaving dollars by layoffs, employing cheaper offshore labor, or replacing senior talent with less experienced junior talent? But layer in sustainability (in this case concerns for social equity), and a world of positive possibilities emerges.

Employees who are passionate about the ideals of sustainability can deliver cost savings in other ways. One method: take seriously the suggestions you receive from the employees on the front lines. Several companies shared stories on this topic. Some of the stories frankly sounded less like actions that came from employee suggestions and more like actions that came from the need to ensure regulatory compliance. But a few stories truly sounded like they arose from employee suggestions. The following story is disguised per interviewee request but is illustrative of how Sustainable Market Leaders link employee suggestions with the pursuit of sustainability.

Based in Thailand, Autotron supplies technology components to PC manufacturers. In 2009 the company designed and implemented a sustainability code of conduct to govern its environmental, labor, health, and safety performance.

According to the company's employee, health, and safety manager, Autotron believes that "the best way to achieve its sustainability goals is through communication and participation of all our employees." This manager shared that the company has seen decreased turnover rates and decreased accident rates since implementing its sustainability code of conduct, saving the company more than $500,000 in employee turnover and accident expenses. In a field where single-digit margins are the norm, a $500,000 decrease in operating expenses is significant.

Creating Tangible and Intangible Value

Sustainable Market Leaders actively seek ways to make their sustainability commitment enhance the value of their hard and soft assets. Whether through modifying their built environment to garner Leadership in Energy and Environmental Design (LEED) certification or altering their logos to communicate their affinity for green ideals, Sustainable Market Leaders tirelessly work to integrate sustainability throughout their balance sheets.

Tangible Assets

The global pursuit of sustainability is opening a temporary window of opportunity for progressive companies to enhance the value of their plant, property, and equipment. According to the U.S. Energy Information Administration, buildings are responsible for nearly half (48 percent) of all greenhouse gas emissions annually. With carbon regulations looming in the United States, commercial building owners know that lowering their buildings' carbon footprints now will lead to lower (carbon emission) expenses in the future.

Consider J. P. Morgan's headquarter building at 270 Park Avenue in New York City. Union Carbide had constructed it in 1961. Manufacturers Hanover bought it in 1978 for $110 million (in 1978 dollars).[11] When Manufacturers Hanover and Chemical Bank merged in 1991, the building became the headquarters for the combined entity. A series of mergers and acquisitions led to J. P. Morgan's ownership of the building, the 104th largest building in the United States.

In 2010 the glass and steel skyscraper between 47th and 48th Streets was undergoing numerous modifications to earn platinum LEED certification, the most demanding LEED certification level. There are many reasons J. P. Morgan chose to take on this expense. The company has embraced the ethos of sustainability and believes that talking the talk with sustainability clients means walking the walk themselves. Less often discussed, though not less valuable, is the belief that "greening" the building will enhance its value.

Is there a basis for this belief? Yes, according to multiple research studies. While some of the studies have sponsorship connections to the green construction industry and thus need to be taken with a grain of salt, others appear completely objective. One such study, conducted by two academics at the Henley Business School at the University of Reading, found LEED buildings should come with a 31 percent premium price relative to non-LEED certified buildings. While the authors note the price premium appears "high for the LEED buildings," they also say, "These premiums are consistent with some previously published results and the mean and median values observed for the data set."[12]

Intangible Assets

In their book, *Invisible Advantage: How Intangibles Are Driving Business Performance*, Jonathan Low and Pam Cohen Kalafut, describe how value "is incorporated in the relationships and reputations a company establishes—with suppliers, with customers, with partners, and with stakeholders of all sorts."[13]

Sustainable Market Leaders seek to turn every little detail into economic advantage. They integrate sustainability with strategy to enhance the drivers of tangible (physical assets) and intangible (assets that cannot be seen or held) value. Sustainable Market Leaders such as Unilever have strengthened venerable brands by first understanding and then amplifying a brand's social contribution while minimizing environmental impact. These same companies have actively reflected on and in several cases changed their corporate logos to communicate their green interests to all observers as a way to attract and retain customers. They have embraced the ideals of transparency to earn back individuals' trust in corporations lost due to the corporate malfeasance of several now-defunct companies. And they have come to understand and are beginning to assign a value to the importance of nurturing and maintaining their portfolio of licenses to operate in local communities.

Brand Equity. Sustainable Market Leaders' efforts to integrate sustainability into their brands are leading to competitive advantages. As Unilever's Santiago Gowland told me:

> The way we look at competitive advantage really is through our ability to nurture and further enhance our brands. When you begin to see social, economic, and environmental elements filtered into the attributes that consumers really value, you can see the power of integrating sustainability into our products and brands. To give an example, when a consumer buys our Lipton tea certified by Rainforest Alliance, what we know from research is that consumers perceive that the care that we put into the production of the raw materials is related to the quality of the product they purchased.
>
> Therefore when we track the equity of that brand through the campaign with Rainforest Alliance, we see that consumers perceive that the quality of the tea is better, that the taste is better, and that the brand is more relevant to them. We have seen all the attributes of a brand equity being enhanced through our sustainability commitments and initiatives. In the

case of Lipton for example we reversed declining market share volumes growth and margins, as a result of the campaign. So you can see how powerful the ethical sourcing dimension of our sustainability strategy was for Lipton.

Similarly when we look at other brands, for example, laundry, the whole strategy of concentration, you can see the connection between sustainability and financial performance. We can see how the concentration strategy literally reduced the cost of conducting our laundry business because concentration has a reduction in energy, packaging, waste, transport, all the costs associated with size. We can also see how it enhanced consumer preference. So what I'm saying is that the single most important lever of competitive advantage for Unilever is the strength of our brands. Sustainability is strengthening this advantage.

This is also quite important for our relationships with our big retailer customers. We've noticed that because big retailers are now taking leadership positions on sustainability, our leadership in this space vis-à-vis our competitors gives us preferred treatment with them. So when customers or retailers want to develop those strategies, Unilever is quite closely working with them, which strengthens the partnership with them, which will then reflect in budgetary terms.

More and more companies are also connecting sustainability with their corporate brand. For example, Marks & Spencer launched Plan A, their portfolio of sustainability commitments and initiatives, in January 2007. Plan A isn't solely internal shorthand; the company has come to view Plan A *as* the basis for their corporate brand. As Adam Elman, head of delivery–Plan A and sustainable business at Marks & Spencer, noted:

> Plan A was always about changing the business, not having a
> team of 200 people on the side of business that was looking
> after it. And that's key to making what we do sustainable, i.e.

making sure that it doesn't stop tomorrow, doesn't stop next
week, it's just the way we do business now.

The effort to connect sustainability and branding extends to
other blue chip companies with market-leading brand equity that
has been built over decades, such as General Electric (GE),
Hitachi, and IBM. GE's tagline—"Imagination at work"—is
reflected in their twin sustainability-oriented business lines: ecomagination and healthymagination (one could envision extensions of the "-magination" brand to include services that target
unmet needs in the education space (edumagination?) for
example). Hitachi is reprioritizing assets and investments around
being a social innovation business—the fusion of sustainable
social infrastructure solutions and intelligent IT—supported by
its brand strategy: "Society changes. Hitachi transforms it." And
IBM's Smarter Planet campaign has won many awards, not to
mention the admiration of clients and competitors alike.

Corporate Logos. Sustainable Market Leaders pay special
attention to every detail of their external communications and
use every detail to their advantage. One lever of these companies' efforts is corporate logos. Logos' ability to communicate the
beliefs and values closely held by the company they represent is
powerful.

Several years ago, a friend pointed out the subliminal arrow
embedded in FedEx's corporate logo. Admittedly it took me a
couple days to really see it. After all, I was trying to turn the tide
of long-term memory—I've seen countless FedEx trucks over the
years. Surely I would have noticed an arrow embedded within a
logo. Only after staring at a FedEx truck for what seemed like an
eternity (likely no more than twenty seconds), I finally noticed
the arrow. Fifteen years later I can't help but notice the arrow
every time I spot a FedEx truck. What is the arrow's significance?
It communicates what the company is about—moving products,
and aspirations, forward.

Consider Kodak. To communicate the company's commitment to sustainability and call attention to its environmentally preferred products and services, Kodak has begun adorning marketing and packaging materials for these products with its new Kodak Cares logo. The company is attaching the new logo to products that help customers manage their environmental footprints, recycle and reuse programs, and initiatives that seek to educate customers about Kodak's environmental programs. One of the first products to receive the internal certification was the Kodak Adaptive Picture Exchange, a photo processing system that uses no water, produces no chemical waste, and uses between 70 and 90 percent less energy than comparable products.

Charles Ruffing, Kodak's director of health, safety, environment, and sustainability, shared the background of the logo's creation:

> So the logo came about because some of our businesses were recognizing that customers were placing more and more value on environmental features. There's a fair number of Kodak products for which third-party-verified eco-logo categories don't exist. So, for example, we can't say we have an EnergyStar commercial printing press because there's no category in EnergyStar for commercial presses. We can't say that there's a Blue Angel photo kiosk because the category doesn't exist. So we were looking for a way that within certain important categories of our products we could call attention to beneficial environmental attributes where a third-party logo didn't exist. We had a marketing team put their heads together which led to the creation of the Kodak Cares logo. (See Figure 3.3.)

While the logo is configured to communicate environmental attributes, Ruffing sees value in one day extending the Kodak Cares ethos to social sustainability as well:

Figure 3.3 New Kodak Cares Logo

Source: Kodak. Reprinted with permission.

When the marketing people started to work on the new logo, they looked at what we'd done before, where we were now, and also how we could introduce something today that we can have room to build on in the future. That's where we came up with the word *care* because care is meant to be more forward looking . . . something we can leverage into a sustainability logo system in the future that reflects more than just environment. So internally we're looking at this maybe as the first piece of something that would grow and then we would have an entire sustainability branding system where Kodak Cares with the leaf might represent the environmental leg, but we could carry through the Kodak Cares terminology with some other emblem to have maybe a social component, a logo for the social component.

Reputation. According to the 2009 Edelman Trust Barometer, individuals' trust of corporations fell off dramatically, from 58 percent of respondents in 2007 to 38 percent in 2008.[14] The implosions of Bear Stearns and Lehman Brothers and the near-nationalization of General Motors, Chrysler, Citigroup, and others, lead to this general decrease.

At the center of these appalling failures is a shocking lack of honesty, integrity, and transparency. As just one example of this well-covered topic, consider the following quote provided by Richard Fuld, CEO of now-defunct Lehman Brothers, during a conference call to preannounce earnings on September 10, 2008: "We are on the right track to put the last two quarters behind us." Five days later, the firm filed for bankruptcy.

Sustainable Market Leaders actively promote transparency as a core value. They view the annual rite of filing responses to environmental and social surveys issued by the Carbon Disclosure Project, Sustainability Asset Management, and KLD Research and Analytics (acquired in 2010 by RiskMetrics Group), among others, as an opportunity to communicate their environmental risks en masse to the investment community. As executives at several Sustainable Market Leaders put it, "If we have the environmental or social data, we share the data."

Local License to Operate. Sustainable Market Leaders nurture and value their licenses to operate in local communities. These companies apply a holistic lens to their interactions with the communities in which they operate—they consider the best interests of local employees, governments, ecosystems, and, at least indirectly, competitors. While philanthropy is a stalwart component of their strategies to protect their licenses to operate, so too are employee volunteerism, environmental stewardship, and actions to support ongoing economic development. These companies develop strategies to improve people's lives in the communities where they do business.

I've often wondered if companies can break down their "goodwill" balance sheet line items into portfolios of local licenses to operate. I imagine the market would reward such transparency. At the very least, a loss of license to operate could be more properly valued by the market and therefore by the company too. Equipped with this information, the company could better determine which local communities to heavily invest in and which, if any, to exit in order to maximize its ability to create business value.

I imagine sooner than later the financial markets will demand greater transparency into the goodwill account on companies' balance sheets. For example, if a global company loses its license to operate in China, the resulting decrease in market value for that company should be quantifiable.

Conclusion

This chapter has shown how Sustainable Market Leaders are creating top-line (increased revenue and increased brand value) and bottom-line (reduced costs and reduced risks) for their stakeholders. These companies have embraced sustainability as a reason to question long-held assumptions about what their customers want and need, and the efficiency of their value chain's activities. Their actions show that integration of sustainability can lead to the creation of measureable value, by enhancing both tangible (products and services) and intangible (brand and reputation) assets.

DIAGNOSTIC

Has your company honestly explored:

Income Statement: Revenue

1. Charging a premium price for the demonstrated total cost of ownership savings your sustainably produced goods provide to end customers?
2. Pursuing and providing new solutions and/or information on your own sustainability activities to
   a. Accelerate your customers' efforts to redesign their "taken for granted" tasks and activities:
      - Replacing wood pallets with plastic pallets within transportation processes (opportunity for chemical companies in particular, but also seaborne transportation companies to show that shipping has a lower carbon footprint than air freight)
      - Sourcing recycled materials for use in manufacturing processes instead of virgin materials (opportunity for any company that either leverages a successful materials recycling system, such as lead batteries or aluminum cans, as well as companies that assist in the recycled materials process, such as lead smelters and bottle recyclers)
      - Serving as a sustainability consultant to your clients in order to search for these hidden opportunities (opportunity for all companies in all industries)
   b. Enable your customers' pursuit of new sustainability activities:
      - Providing tools and/or advanced insights to support customers' efforts to measure and report their owned and contracted carbon footprints, as well as other environmental and/or social activities (opportunity for all companies in all industries, with emphasis on heavy carbon emitting industries)
      - Supporting new market entry efforts, such as, providing low-cost, recyclable kegs or other types of containers to support manufacturers' efforts to combat illicit substitute goods with properly sourced and affordable, sustainably produced goods
   c. Making available your efforts (and plans) to address environmental and social inefficiencies in your own operations as answers to customers' request for proposal-based environmentally savvy questions

Income Statement: Costs

1. Investing to reduce your carbon emissions?

    a. Have you mapped out your carbon emissions by supply chain step (for example, manufacturing, logistics, packaging)?

    b. Have you benchmarked your emissions-per-step versus your peers?

    c. What would happen if companies with lower carbon emissions per unit produced "baked in" their per unit carbon emissions into their product price and disclosed their carbon emissions clearly, transparently, and simply on their products? Would you be at an advantage or disadvantage given your carbon footprint?

2. Lowering your usage of fossil fuels by

    a. Investing in developing your own renewable energy sources (for example, building a biofuel facility and using the waste from your manufacturing processes as source matter for the facility)?

    b. Employing energy efficient data centers, employee laptops, and/or other mobile technology?

3. Employing fresh approaches to tried-and-true logistics activities, such as

    a. Using lighter weight pallets and/or shipping containers that use cradle-to-cradle manufacturing processes?

4. Hedging against the rising cost of raw materials by exploiting the growing recycling trend?

Balance Sheet: Hard Assets, such as Plant, Property, and Equipment

1. Are you maximizing the imprisoned assets tied up in your own built environment by greening your buildings to meet LEED certification?

Balance Sheet: Brand

1. Are you protecting your brand value by monitoring social media chatter about real or implied indiscretions within your value or supply chains?

2. Are you exposing your company to greenwash accusations by aggressively pushing the envelope on your sustainability claims?

3. Are you able to quantify the percentage of your goodwill account that is dependent on your portfolio of licenses to operate?

Balance Sheet: Trust

1. Are you rebuilding individuals' trust in your company by

   a. Associating your company with organizations, such as NGOs, that the general public trusts?

   b. Disclosing material environmental and/or social inefficiencies through regular sustainability reporting?

Balance Sheet: License to Operate

1. Are you taking the temperature of your company's relationships with the local communities in which it operates?

2. When was the last time your company sought input from the local communities in which it operates?

Part Two

HOW TO CREATE VALUE IN YOUR ORGANIZATION

4

CRAFTING SUSTAINABILITY STRATEGY

In Part One we explored how sustainability creates value for stakeholders. In Part Two, beginning with this chapter, we explore how the CLEAR Model (refer to Figure I.2 in the Introduction for a complete diagram of the CLEAR Model) enables companies to embrace sustainability as a way to differentiate from their peers, craft high-performance strategies, and maximize the value they create for stakeholders. In this chapter we explore how Sustainable Market Leaders sharpen their corporate and competitive strategies through their decision to embrace sustainability.

Strategy Formulation

In the Preface to this book, I talked about David Cohen, a dear mentor of mine whom I had the privilege to meet in 1996. David's nurturing led me to develop a passion for strategy. After my time working with Andersen Consulting, I went to the Wharton School at the University of Pennsylvania to earn an MBA in strategic management.

My favorite strategy class was Management 701: Strategic Planning and Controls, taught by Gabriel Szulanski (now a distinguished strategy professor at INSEAD). The class focused on two critical areas of strategy: the various schools of strategy thinking and the strategy-planning approach many companies pursue. After we completed our study of strategy giants such as Michael Porter, Gary Hamel, Henry Mintzberg, and Costas Markides, we actively debated the question of whether the best

Table 4.1 Professor Gabriel Szulanski's Approach to Strategy Formulation

Step	Description
Look inside the organization	Gather, analyze, and communicate the organization's initiatives' status and results to date through metrics and analytics
Look outside the organization	Gather, interpret, and communicate relevant occurrences in the external environment through competitive intelligence and market research
Frame the problem	The collective words and images the organization uses to describe its strategy, challenges, goals, and aspirations
Strategy-making entity	The people involved in the strategy formulation process and how these people interact
Develop alternatives	Appetite for and availability of creative thinking, brainstorming, and influence of one or more organization-specific factors over the strategy formulation process
Select strategy	How the organization selects its strategies from among the proposed alternatives

strategies came about from deliberate planning or simply emerged. (I believe the answer is somewhere in the middle). We then explored strategic-planning approaches, eventually focusing on six steps in the strategy-crafting process (see Table 4.1).

When I started my sustainability management research, I was excited to learn more about each Sustainable Market Leader's approach to sustainability strategy. Would I discover, as we had discussed in Szulanski's class, that every company deliberately plans a sustainability strategy or that such a strategy simply emerged out of its dedication to timeless management principles? Assuming sustainability strategy was formulated, what processes do the companies use? And how close would this process, on the whole, be to the six steps we studied and actively debated in class?

With this goal in mind, I dedicated a significant portion of each company interview to a consistent set of questions about the company's approach to sustainability strategy. I learned three things from these interviews. First, every company mentioned a surprisingly similar need for such a strategy. Second, each company subscribed primarily to the "deliberate" school of strategy. And third, the stories and opinions shared by the interviewees painted a sustainability strategy formulation maturity timeline. This chapter covers each of these findings.

Before we dive into the findings, a couple more notes from the interviews are worth a brief mention. The one constant I heard throughout my research is that becoming more mature in every aspect of sustainability management relies on an evolutionary, not a revolutionary, mindset. Said simply, a company cannot go from not having a sustainability strategy to integrating sustainability into corporate and competitive strategy-planning processes overnight. Put aside the obvious learning curve aspect of such a leap. Of at least equal importance is the need to bring skeptics along for the sustainability journey. Move too fast, and the skeptics will feel that a sustainability commitment is being forced upon them. Move too slowly, and the skeptics will find reasons to further justify their personal doubts. By moving through the sustainability strategy maturity timeline at a measured yet forward-looking, pace, sustainability managers have a greater likelihood of bringing their organization's skeptics on board as at least neutral parties if not, ultimately, additional (and welcomed) adherents of sustainability-infused corporate and competitive strategy.

Sustainability Strategy Formulation

United Parcel Service (UPS) provides a clear example of how Sustainable Market Leaders formulate sustainability strategy. UPS is well regarded for its systematic, data-driven approach to management and execution for reasons that are well apparent. After all, its workforce of 408,000 employees delivers more than 15 million packages a day to more than 6 million customers in more than 200 countries and territories worldwide.[1]

The company has approached sustainability with the same entrepreneurship, precision, and passion demonstrated when cofounders Jim Casey and Claude Ryan delivered their first messages in 1907. Indeed, according to Ed Rogers, global strategy manager at UPS, the company's oft-lauded sustainability efforts grew from an informal beginning:

> In 2007 I was asked to be the strategy guy that would work with a handful of other people to formalize our sustainability effort. At the time, our sustainability efforts were conducted on a well-intentioned, but disconnected basis by many different functions. Talent management was championed by HR. Society investments and volunteerism was championed by the UPS Foundation, which is our charitable arm. Environmental management was led by our plant engineering function. Activities related to economics and new products and services were led by a combination of finance, marketing, and new product development.

Rogers's insight from this beginning was that UPS needed to make a connection between sustainability and corporate strategy. Specifically, the company looked inside to grasp what sustainability meant to UPS and looked outside to spot changes in the regulatory environment that colors their markets. Rogers explained:

> I was asked to work with my colleagues to think about how we could lay out and communicate our sustainability strategy at UPS. There were less than a dozen of us that were involved in it at that point and no one was full time. These were all kind of additional duties that people were taking on. We met and discussed sustainability issues regularly, mainly focused on how UPS would produce next year's sustainability report. As this small group kept meeting, we kept hearing about emerging legislation like carbon cap and trade, we realized that

sustainability was poised to have a significant impact on industry pretty soon. We needed to get out in front of it.

UPS's insight led the company to frame sustainability in terms of risk. In response UPS decided to appoint full-time resources to sustainability management. Rogers worked closely with these colleagues and related functions to better understand sustainability and its related impacts and challenges. Rogers recalled:

> In 2008 UPS appointed full time resources to sustainability. While I remained in our global strategy function, we had a core of folks, primarily in our engineering group, that were put together to do that. During the year I worked with both this group and also a range of different functions around the company to understand all of the things that looked or felt like the sustainability space—metrics, tactics, principles, and strategies were documented. I met with many people, I reviewed everything that we had online regarding sustainability. I read both our old sustainability reports and our competitors' sustainability reports. And I attended various sustainability conferences to get a better understanding and appreciation for what are the key themes, the big issues, and the most successful tactics companies were using to embrace sustainability.

Rogers soon had an impressive collection of content. In need of a rubric to effectively communicate this information, he turned to a strategic management framework UPS had previously used to support strategic decision making to organize the information from his research:

> I pulled this all together and tried to think of a framework to organize all of this in a coherent, cohesive manner. Back in the late '90s, I had been involved in the development of what we call strategic frameworks. UPS functions and business units

used these frameworks to lay out their mission and vision, and then determine their key principles, strategies, and metrics, as well as the projects and initiatives that needed to be done. Using that blueprint seemed like a good way to capture and logically organize all of the activity that was going on related to sustainability and lay it out in a logical manner. So we fleshed these actions out as a way to catalog all the stuff that was going on. Then we highlighted things that we weren't doing but other companies were. Finally we concluded that we should consider making sustainability part of our strategy.

By using the long-established strategy framework to organize and articulate UPS's sustainability interests and efforts, Rogers was able to present facts, gaps, and alternative ideas to fill these gaps to the sustainability management team appointed to develop UPS's sustainability strategy:

I wanted to boil all of this content down to a set of core principles for sustainability. I thought if I could show how they relate to our mission, strategy, and performance, then people would get behind sustainability. I wanted to choose a language that was familiar to UPS'ers, one that didn't sound too "consultant-y." By then we had what we called a sustainability working committee, which was a group of about twenty people from different functions. We met monthly to review the progress of each person's sustainability tasks and activities. I brought my draft versions of those principles and the frameworks to those meetings and we spent time reviewing and refining those. Then I held separate breakout sessions with smaller subgroups of our working committee.

The installation of a sustainability management oversight committee led to the selection of a sustainability strategy consistent with UPS's core strategies and performance metrics.

Also in 2008 we had established a sustainability steering committee which included about a half dozen people from our management committee, and some of their direct reports, some key function heads. This committee met quarterly. So I brought a draft version of what turned out to be our sustainability principles and frameworks to this senior group for their review. By the end of 2008 these principles and frameworks were approved, signed off, and copyrighted. Then we finally revealed that strategy, the frameworks, and the principles in our 2009 sustainability report. We have since populated all of that information into our software system that we use for managing and coordinating all of the sustainability efforts here at UPS.

The Need for Sustainability Strategy

Sustainable Market Leaders clearly see the need for a sustainability strategy. To learn more about one Sustainable Market Leader's inherent need for sustainability strategy, I traveled to Beaverton, Oregon, home to the fabled campus of Nike. Set among larger-than-life banners of star athletes are contemporary buildings bearing the names of these athletes. To the left of the Mia Hamm building, and directly across from the Pete Sampras building, is the Jerry Rice building, home to many Nike executives, including Dan Cherian of Nike's Sustainable Business and Innovation team.

Before I met with Dan, I had the privilege of interviewing him twice by phone. Though I greatly enjoyed our conversations, nothing could have prepared me for just how passionate Dan is about sustainability as a platform for growth. Our conversation lasted a little over an hour, yet felt like five minutes. During our conversation I asked Dan to help me better understand companies' need for sustainability strategy. His reply:

Today, no global company can operate without a clear
sustainability strategy—the loud demand and expectation for
one's customers, employees, shareholders, regulators, and
partners cannot be ignored. A company's sustainability
strategy has to truly reflect, embody, and build on the
company's values, aspirations, and core business strategy. A
sustainability strategy created in isolation and then forcibly
connected to corporate strategy and mission will stand out as a
sore thumb. For many industry-leading companies, the
sustainability strategy and the growth and innovation strategy
are one and the same.

A sustainability strategist has to start with corporate
strategy first but know how to not get distracted by near-term
priorities and projects. Sustainability strategies work on the
longer horizon—they are more structural and can be disruptive.
Thus, one needs to think about the basics like, what are the
drivers of my business? What are the long-term challenges and
growth opportunities for my business? And where is it getting
disrupted? From there you can start framing it.

As he described the need for a formulated sustainability strategy, Cherian also described the need for that strategy to ultimately emanate from planning exercises. The next section of the
chapter covers the tools most often employed by Sustainable
Market Leaders to formulate sustainability strategy.

Effective Tools for the "Deliberate" School of Sustainability Strategy Formulation

Few if any companies have the luxury of developing from scratch
an infrastructure to formulate sustainability strategy. The need
to solve some value chain crisis or to capitalize on employees'
grassroots passions typically leads companies to install portions
of a sustainability strategy–creating process. Usually these actions
include setting sustainability-related values, enacting certain

Figure 4.1 Typical Materiality Assessment Process

Determine Issues to Consider	Conduct Interviews	Prioritize Issues of Materiality
• Who are key stakeholders? • Which sustainability issues should the company consider?	• Interview executives • Interview stakeholders	• Plot materiality issues on graph • Set priority of materiality issues

policies or becoming a signatory to one or more well-intended (and effective) sustainability-related voluntary agreements.

Despite the institutional memory that arises from such actions, companies can learn from and install the same tools and approaches employed by Sustainable Market Leaders to frame the problem, look inside the organization, look outside the organization, develop an effective sustainability strategy–making entity, develop alternatives, and ultimately craft a sustainability strategy. Perhaps the most effective tool companies employ to address the first three steps in the strategy formulation process outlined in Figure 4.1 is the completion of a holistic (and brutally honest) materiality assessment. Simply put, a materiality assessment enables a company to prioritize investment in and pursuit of a set of sustainability's myriad issues. Typically, the materiality assessment consists of three activities, each with at least two tasks.

This task enables companies to create a custom definition of sustainability for their organizations and unique sets of stakeholders, illustrated by a set of environmental and social issues that are most relevant to both the companies and their stakeholders.

To illustrate the materiality assessment process conducted by a Sustainable Market Leader, consider the development of Hitachi's process. Based in Tokyo, Japan, Hitachi opened its doors in 1910, originally focused on producing power generation equipment. While Hitachi still maintains a robust power systems business, the company has diversified into an electronics and business services organization. Sustainability touches and colors many aspects of Hitachi's business—from the carbon footprint of its power systems to the development and maintenance of its portfolio of licenses to operate in a mosaic of local communities.

As recalled by Brian Larnerd, Hitachi's senior manager of corporate social responsibility (CSR), wrapping Hitachi's arms around the range of sustainability issues most material to its business was critical to the development of the company's sustainability strategy:

> We set out our first three-year CSR roadmap that went from April of 2006 to April 2010. Our goal at the end of the three-year period was to be a leading global CSR company. One of my tasks was to identify what that meant. And a separate but related task was to better understand how we would achieve this goal. We have a very small team; I work with a colleague in Japan at the Hitachi headquarters level. So we recognized the need to work with an external third party to gather outside perspectives and insights. So in collaboration with Business for Social Responsibility, my colleague and I put together a strategy to set us down the course of creating a world class approach to what we're calling strategic CSR, where we integrate CSR into our business strategy and focus on the issues that matter the most to us as a business over the long term.

This is where the materiality assessment comes into play. Larnerd continued:

> The materiality assessment is about identifying the most important issues to our stakeholders while also analyzing the influence these issues have over our long-term business success. We wanted to revert back to our roots.

So our materiality assessment has been one of, "CSR is at the very heart of Hitachi. And it's not something that we need to talk about but it's something that every Hitachi employee needs to understand and needs to know." We put in place a mechanism to better understand what are the most important issues facing our stakeholders. First we asked who are our most important stakeholders? We decided that we needed to prioritize those issues and then see how they influence our long-term business success.

Once Hitachi decided to conduct a materiality assessment to inform the development of its CSR strategy, the next task was to prioritize the issues arising from the materiality assessment. To identify issues to assess for materiality, Hitachi, along with outside experts, referred to the indices used by major socially responsible investing and sustainability investor surveys, as well as global standards. The company then summarized these elements into forty-seven categories and set five levels to be reached for each category. Larnerd continued:

First we sought to understand, "What CSR issues matter the most at the corporate level, at the global level for us?" We focused on the very big issues. Issues we looked at include public policy, sustainability solutions, diversity, waste, nuclear waste, e-waste, bribery, and corruption, among others. Then we sought to understand what CSR issues matter the most at our business segment level. Doing so helped better inform our decision makers as to what are the highest potential market and revenue opportunities resulting from sustainability. So in the end it's not to make this a CSR cost or try to minimize risks per se, but actually to enable business growth and profitability and long-term sustainability of the business and at the same time contribute to social and environmental progress for future generations.

Figure 4.2 Materiality Assessment Template

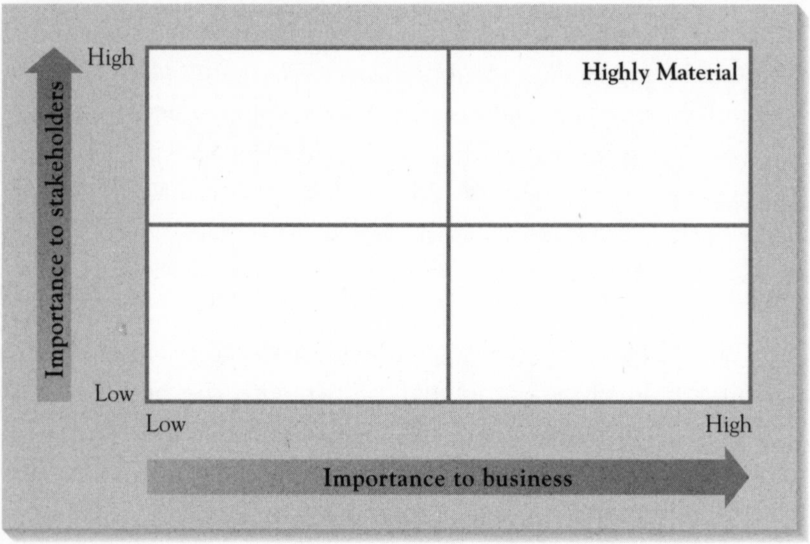

Sustainable Market Leaders such as Hitachi employ a remarkably similar model to determine the importance of evaluated material issues. The model consists of two axes—typically the x-axis represents the importance of the issue to the company's performance, while the y-axis represents the importance of the issue to the company's stakeholders (see Figure 4.2).

Again Brian Larnerd:

> We had formed the stakeholder side decisions from stakeholder engagement, various activities like that. Understanding what are trends, local community needs, things linked to millennium development goals, et cetera. Then on the business success axis we linked some of those stakeholder CSR issues to our business criteria, such as revenue growth, reputation, products and services, synergies, business risks, et cetera. We completed our analysis by looking at the upper right corner box as, "That's where we need to focus our CSR strategy to inform the business strategy as well as our communications strategy on the issues that matter the most to us right now."

Figure 4.3 Hitachi's Materiality Assessment

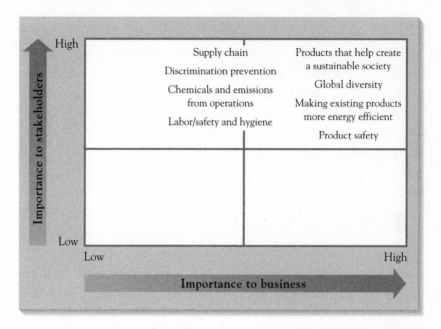

Figure 4.3 illustrates the result of Hitachi's CSR materiality assessment.

A proper materiality assessment can inform the design of a company's sustainability strategy. That is, the outcome of the materiality assessment—a prioritization of issues deemed highly material to *both* the company and the company's stakeholders—naturally leads to a series of performance and strategy questions. What actions are we taking to promote global diversity within our value chain? And how does consistently achieving global diversity relate to our financial performance and our competitive positioning? Larnerd described Hitachi's approach:

> Once the materiality assessment was complete, we worked with
> our various corporate functions, our corporate strategy team,
> and our top management to use the outcome to better inform
> the competitive strategy decision-making process.

One step in this process was to conduct an assessment of Hitachi's current CSR performance at the department level. Indeed, most Sustainable Market Leaders require that their various departments benchmark and document their current performance within each of the identified highly material issues.

Let's follow our Hitachi example to see how this benchmarking process works. Informed by its materiality assessment, Hitachi tested and refined a series of eight policies to codify its mostly closely held sustainability values and goals. This assessment clarified strengths, weaknesses, and desired CSR direction, as well as the results the company hopes to achieve.

Senior management required operations throughout the business to conduct a materiality benchmarking assessment in both 2008 and 2009. According to the company, discussions were held several times with major Hitachi Group companies during the assessment's development to ensure that all companies in the Hitachi Group use this tool. An application manual was created to demonstrate the effective use of the tool. In addition, the manual lays out scoring criteria and explains how the tool can be applied, depending on each individual Hitachi business and operation.

In 2008, the results within each business unit served as a baseline. Larnerd and his team used this baseline to set short-term CSR improvement goals for each unit. Then, in 2009, each business unit again analyzed its performance along each highly material issue. Equipped with these results, Hitachi has been able to develop a set of initiatives to further enhance its business units' sustainability performance.

Integrating Sustainability with Strategy

When I was fourteen I had surgery on both knees. I set a goal to recover in time to run for my school's track and field team. As I started my recovery, my uncle, a well-regarded sportswriter, sent me a book on jogging with the inscription:

Before you can run, you have to walk. Before you can walk, you have to crawl. Get going!

I often thought about this inscription during the interviews as company after company described to me their sustainability strategy formulation processes. Many companies noted their strategies had modest beginnings: one or more employees seeking ways to "green" their local offices, for instance. One giant financial services firm shared that at one time there were "well over a hundred of these local level efforts under way . . . effective individually, but costly collectively." When pressed why these efforts were costly, the interviewee (who requested anonymity both for his company and himself) confided that "a good amount of these efforts were redundant. . . . Employees recreated the wheel instead of searching for like-minded colleagues to learn from . . . and ultimately the lack of a coherent sustainability plan from senior management deflated these employees' motivation and passion for sustainability-oriented change."

The UPS story at the beginning of this chapter demonstrates the three stages of sustainability strategy maturation Sustainable Market Leaders have worked through to integrate sustainability into corporate and competitive strategy. These three stages form the continuum shown in Figure 4.4.

Figure 4.4 Sustainability Strategy Maturity Continuum

No Strategy	Sustainability Strategy	Sustainability Infused Strategy
• Loose collection of grassroots actions • Well-intended, uncoordinated actions	• Sustainability vision, supported by planned activities • Separate from corporate and competitive strategies	• Sustainability strategy *is* the company's corporate strategy • Material sustainability issues incorporated in planning efforts

At one end of this continuum (Stage 1) is a set of uncoordinated, one-off environmental and/or social sustainability efforts designed and completed in a grassroots style by well-intentioned employees. In the middle of the maturity continuum (Stage 2) are companies' efforts to craft and carry out sustainability strategies developed in addition to traditional corporate and competitive strategy plans. Integration of sustainability into corporate and competitive strategy-planning processes is on the right side of the maturity continuum (Stage 3).

Going from Stage 1 to Stage 2

Moving from Stage 1 to Stage 2 along the maturity continuum is a no-brainer. The benefits of doing so—a vision of what the company wants to achieve that provides employees with direction while mitigating risks the company sees on the horizon—far outweigh the challenges.

The majority of Sustainable Market Leaders called upon their sustainability teams to provide a structure for and facilitate the process of sustainability strategy formulation. Recognizing that the strategy would require the cooperation of business units, functions, and regional operations, these companies installed sustainability committees (I explore these in detail in Chapter Five) to be charged with the responsibility for selecting among strategy alternatives to craft and set their companies' sustainability strategies.

Formulating such a strategy provides companies with both sustainability visions to guide their journeys and roadmaps of the risks that may develop into roadblocks.

Sustainability Vision. The sustainability vision that companies create during Stage 2 clearly spells out what sustainability means to the company. Brian Larnerd at Hitachi underscored this point:

In our three-year plan ending in 2010, we put a goalpost out
there that says we wanted to be a leading global CSR company.
So I set out to identify what that meant.

Once the company can articulate what their sustainability
strategy is, their employees will be better enabled to act in a
coordinated, thoughtful way to carry out this strategy. Arlin
Wasserman, Sodexo's vice president of sustainability and corporate social responsibility, concretized the rationale for creating a
sustainability strategy:

> Think about grassroots sustainability efforts as having a
> thousand people doing modest work. Having a sustainability
> plan enables these same folks to do the best work they can
> while increasing the likelihood that those people will make
> better sustainability-related decisions on a daily basis.

Goal Setting and Risk Mitigation. The second benefit of
having a sustainability strategy is found in the form of traditional
goal setting. Sustainable Market Leaders employ the findings
from their materiality assessment to set goals within each
identified material issue, much like goals for market share and
penetration are set.

To develop these goals, the company may encourage each of
its business units to self-assess its current impacts within and
compliance with each of the issues deemed material. For example,
let's say ethical sourcing is identified as a material issue for both
the company and its stakeholders. The company might set a goal,
to be achieved within three years, of sourcing 100 percent of its
materials through suppliers deemed and verified as being fully
compliant with the United Nations Global Compact's Ten
Principles. During the goal-setting phase, one or more of the
company's business units might discover that one of their key
suppliers conducts business in regions without well-established,

nonautocratic governments, increasing the likelihood of under-the-table payments somewhere in the value chain. The act of setting a goal of ethical sourcing will have led the company to identify a potential risk, increasing the likelihood that this risk can be mitigated before it evolves into a public relations headache.

Australia & New Zealand Banking Group (ANZ Banking Group) understands the importance of having a sustainability vision for its employees to work toward. To wit, ANZ Banking Group actively seeks the counsel of employees and other stakeholders to develop this vision. The following story highlights the importance of working with employees to set sustainability strategy.

In 2009, ANZ Banking Group set out to develop a new corporate responsibility framework to support and strengthen the company's business strategy, brand, and values, and ensure the company was making a significant and focused contribution to the world. To begin, ANZ Banking Group commissioned research across a sample of its key markets—Australia, Indonesia, and China—which showed that despite different cultures, there are strong similarities in consumer expectations of responsible corporations. Being honest and transparent, treating employees fairly, providing responsible products and services, and contributing to local community issues and causes were consistently identified as threshold issues. Environmental concerns varied across countries and related to local challenges such as fresh water shortages, water sanitation, air quality, and traffic congestion.

ANZ Banking Group sought considerable input from stakeholders ranging from customers to employees to shareholders. Specifically, the company reviewed findings from extensive focus groups undertaken with more than 1,300 customers and 250 staff to develop their new global brand. This brand research found that regardless of age, gender, or geography, customers want their bank and bank products to be people focused and uncomplicated. ANZ Banking Group also researched the agendas of governments, local and international nongovernmental organizations (NGOs), and multilateral organizations to understand their respective views on the most pressing economic, social, and environmental issues and opportunities facing specific countries and the region more generally. The company considered their medium- to long-term strategic priorities and assessed where they, as a bank, could make the most constructive contribution.

ANZ Banking Group reports that engagement with local stakeholders in some key markets to develop a CR framework that would resonate with its employees, customers, communities, governments, and regulators was a critical ingredient to its framework development efforts. This became one of the most significant engagement exercises undertaken by the bank. In addition to day-to-day stakeholder conversations, ANZ Banking Group consulted nearly 600 people through face-to-face workshops conducted in seven countries as part of this process.

The company listened to stakeholders' concerns about their own lives and communities and their expectations for a bank that shares their world. According to the company, several consistent themes emerged:

- As the global financial crisis played out in each of [ANZ Banking Group's] markets, all stakeholders urged ANZ Banking Group to grow responsibly by treating [its] customers and employees fairly and with care; providing the right products and services to meet customer needs; and to take greater account of economic, social, and environmental issues in our business decisions.

- Education and employment opportunities are key to changing people's lives and are highly valued by individuals and in the development priorities of governments throughout the region.

- Bridging rural and urban economic and social divides is perhaps the most significant challenge for many governments and communities, particularly in Asia and the Pacific. Banking access and financial inclusion are key strategies where [it] can make a difference.

- Supporting and building financial resilience, capability, and well-being among customers and improving access to mainstream products and services for underserved and unbanked communities was considered a key corporate responsibility for banks in every market.

- Improving urban sustainability is an important priority for governments and communities and, increasingly, [its] customers live in urban centers and are faced with congestion, air quality, and sanitation challenges.

The material issues raised through this research and stakeholder engagement process were then analyzed and mapped against ANZ Banking Group's business objectives, helping it to articulate its purpose in society and CR priorities. Today ANZ Banking Group's Corporate Responsibility Framework provides global direction for the company's initiatives and investments, while allowing flexibility to suit the specific needs of diverse geographic locations and markets.

Going from Stage 2 to Stage 3

More and more Sustainable Market Leaders are eschewing the creation of a sustainability strategy by instead integrating sustainability into their corporate and competitive strategy-planning processes. Indeed Sustainable Market Leaders such as Starbucks, 3M, GlaxoSmithKline (GSK), Centrica, and Nike have successfully completed this integration. Their rationale is best summed up by Ben Packard, vice president of global responsibility at Starbucks:

> At Starbucks, sustainability and strategy are now integrated at
> the strategic-planning level. The Global Responsibility strategy

is a component of the enterprise strategy and driven at that
enterprise, strategic-planning and annual operating planning
level, because the bigger costs around driving either changes in
supply chain or operations or global development occur outside
of my budget. So it's an integrated model driven by a strategic
plank in our enterprise strategy.

I think there is a danger when companies conduct separate
strategic-planning exercises on sustainability and corporate
strategy because anything that doesn't make its way into
corporate and/or competitive strategy plans usually is left off
the operating plans table as well.

Jean Sweeney, vice president of environmental, health, and
safety at 3M, echoed Packard's statement:

We don't view our sustainability strategy as being a separate
strategy from our business strategy. It is integral to our
business strategy. Our business strategy for many decades
has included our environmental performance, our social
responsibilities, and certainly our economic responsibilities
including governance of the company. As we build business
strategy, we always are looking at what market trends are
taking place, the megatrends and the smaller trends that are
happening with our specific customers.

The desire to integrate sustainability with corporate strategy
is shared worldwide. Consider GlaxoSmithKline. The global
pharmaceutical company views sustainability and strategy as one
and the same. Julia King, GlaxoSmithKline's vice president of
corporate responsibility, explained GSK's view of corporate
responsibility as all-encompassing:

It's about running our business in a responsible way. So that's
every aspect of the business and it's absolutely central to the

strategy because if you don't run a business in a responsible way, it isn't sustainable. So sustainability isn't an add-on point for us, it's got to be a part of the way you run the business. And it doesn't matter what aspect of the business you're talking about. So it's all very intimately linked and we don't believe you can really separate corporate responsibility from the mainstream strategy of the business. We don't believe you should have a separate sustainability strategy. So if you're looking at your sales and marketing strategy, it has to be sustainable, part of that is making it sustainable. We don't have a separate sustainability strategy.

Integrating sustainability into corporate strategy can lead to powerful value creation opportunities. Such is the case at Centrica, as Amelia Knott described:

Our CR vision is to be the most trusted energy company leading the move to a low-carbon future. The trust element covers securing energy supplies, delivering high-quality customer service, health and safety, and how we look after our people. It's because we're working to build that trust that we can then take steps towards leading the industry and our customers towards more low-carbon energy-efficient solutions.

Developing a clear narrative to explain how all the different facets of CR support our business operations has helped to integrate them into our corporate strategy. In February 2010 we announced new corporate strategic priorities, underpinned by a commitment to provide energy for a low-carbon world. This is even more explicit for British Gas (one of Centrica's four business units) which has a strategic priority to grow British Gas, leading the transition to low carbon homes and business.

Dan Cherian at Nike is actively seeking ways to make such a powerful connection between sustainability and strategy. One of his tools is to draw a two-by-two table. Label one axis "tangible importance to the business." Label the other side "ability to do anything about it." So what companies usually end up pursuing is stuff which companies think they can do—largely alone or with their known universe of suppliers and partners. The gold nuggets for sustainability strategy are the things which are identified as critically important but ignored by business units as something they cannot do anything about.

The road to sustainability integration is difficult because there isn't an off-the-shelf approach to guide this integration. But the level of difficulty hasn't stopped Sustainable Market Leaders currently in Stage 2 to seek ways to achieve Stage 3 maturity. Consider Charles Ruffing at Kodak:

How to integrate sustainability with established strategic-planning efforts has been an important area of focus for me over the past six months or so. Our operations council at Kodak, which is chaired by our president and COO and includes his direct reports who run the corporate and competitive strategy process for our businesses, has asked me in several times now to brainstorm ways to more closely integrate this kind of sustainability thinking with our competitive strategies. And I think we're making some great inroads now. Because a lot of the businesses that we're in, especially our commercial printing business, we're seeing sustainability as necessary in the life blood of the business.

For example, the commercial printing business is about putting images on paper and certainly there's a counter-current in society with a message of "Go green and don't buy the dead tree edition of the magazine." Or, "Get an e-reader, it's better for the environment." And we happen to believe that from a full life cycle perspective, electronic display is not better in all instances.

There are legitimate applications for paper-based printing output. I hope to get a copy of your book in hard copy, perhaps printed on a Kodak press of some kind. And we don't sell books. Our customers who buy our presses sell books. And they really look to us to help them understand forest certification issues, proper use of paper and recycling issues, ability to target mail pieces to customers more specifically rather than printing a million pieces and sending 90 percent of the population something that they're not interested in. And digital printing technologies which we and some of our competitors market enable that more-targeted printing to be more facile. So especially on our commercial side of the business there's a lot of talk about sustainability needing to be one of the key components of our corporate and competitive strategies.

Another factor that makes this transition difficult is the danger of not having a clear sustainability strategy, as articulated by Frank Mantero, GE's director of corporate responsibility:

At times, it's hard for employees to identify that we have a strong CSR position, because for them it's inculcated in the culture that GE exists to solve problems. "Guess what? We're going to make money but we're also going to solve problems while we make money. We're going to engage on really tough topics." That was Edison's vision when he founded the company more than a hundred years ago and that's why 300,000 people work here. That's a core part of the culture in a company like this, not a stand-alone program.

So when somebody asks an employee externally, "What's GE's CSR strategy or what do we do around CSR?" sometimes it's easier for them to identify a philanthropic or volunteering program as the definition of CSR because that is more tangible to them. Frankly, many external stakeholders still define CSR as philanthropy or volunteerism. The opportunity is then to position philanthropy and volunteerism programs as core components (not sole) of an overall CSR strategy.

Cultural Adoption of Sustainability into the Mission-Critical Thinking of the Company. Cultural adoption of sustainability into the daily thinking of senior and junior employees alike is an essential ingredient in the recipe of progressing from Stage 2 to Stage 3. Dr. Eckhard Koch, vice president of BASF's Sustainability Strategy Center, describes such cultural adoption:

> We deeply believe that a business such as ours cannot be successful in the long term if we do not act responsibly towards the environment and society. Therefore, sustainability is an integral part of our strategy and we act accordingly.

But how do Sustainable Market Leaders ensure that sustainability becomes a part of a company's culture? One tactic many of these exemplars use is connecting sustainability to the heritage of their company. This is a tactic being employed by Brian Larnerd and his colleagues at Hitachi:

> The effort to achieve our sustainability vision has led us to ask "Who are we as a company?" 2010 is our centennial anniversary. In setting the corporate and sustainability strategy and the vision for our company, we looked back to who we were and how we were founded. We rediscovered that we're rooted in these principles of sustainability. We reminded our executives that this is who we are.
>
> For us as a company it's about contributing to society through our superior products and technology and helping. And our history is rooted in that. And we carry that forward. We haven't really banged our chest and flaunted the successes that we've achieved. We've done it in a very humble manner. Now we wanted to maintain that approach because a lot companies are bragging about what they do and a lot of greenwashing out there. But this is something, that being a sustainable company is something we've always been. And we wanted to remind first

our executives, "That's who we are." Sustainability is the very heart of Hitachi. And it's not something that we need to talk about but it's something that every Hitachi employee needs to understand and needs to know.

Decentralization. A key step along the transition to Stage 3 is placing the accountability for sustainability planning and results in the hands of the company's business unit, function, and regional managers. Doing so further encourages these "managers in the weeds" to seek ways to integrate sustainability with strategy.

But this is not an easy step to take. Indeed, nearly 80 percent of the interviewees cited this step as their most difficult along the maturation process. The primary cause for this difficulty? Helping these managers realize that sustainability is not synonymous with altruism but rather with business opportunity. Ben Packard at Starbucks explained why his company modified its traditional CSR language to terms that are more familiar to business leaders:

> We engineered a very deliberate language change and we went
> through a very painful process of picking the things that are
> absolutely core to us, making very hard decisions about things
> that we were going to let go and things we were going to stop
> doing. And core to the transformation agenda was being a
> leader in ethical sourcing, environmental stewardship, and
> community involvement. Our business doubled down on
> something that had always been core to the vision and mission,
> but did it in a way that recognized it was essential to our future
> success.

Frank Mantero summed up the level of integration achieved in Stage 3 like this:

> When people ask us what is our corporate citizenship strategy,
> it's very easy at GE because we do have the proof points to say

that our corporate citizenship strategy is our business strategy. Jeff Immelt, our CEO, talks about solving the world's most complex problems or leveraging our resources to engage on health care and energy debates. We also engage with governments and civil society on solving some of these problems, on bringing to bear our employees and their resources to engage locally. It is our citizenship strategy.

Conclusion

Crafting strategy has long been considered more of an art than a science by companies, industry observers, and academics alike. Integrating sustainability into the strategy mix further complicates this nonstandard process. But there are certain tasks and activities Sustainable Market Leaders are completing in order to integrate sustainability with strategy. These companies are committing themselves to a journey to become sustainable, conducting a materiality assessment to determine the points of intersection between what they and their stakeholders care most about, and ultimately seeking ways to weave these material issues into long established strategy-crafting processes at the enterprise and business unit levels.

DIAGNOSTIC

1. What stage of integration maturity best defines your company's sustainability strategy right now?

   Stage 1
   - Your company does not have a formalized sustainability strategy.
   - Some of your employees have organized local-level, grassroots efforts to encourage your company to become more environmentally and/or socially sustainable.

   Stage 2
   - Your company has a documented and communicated sustainability strategy or vision that is wholly separate from your company's corporate and competitive strategies.

   Stage 3
   - Your company's corporate and competitive strategies *are* your sustainability strategies and vice versa. In other words, you have integrated your sustainability strategy into your strategic plans so that you no longer have a sustainability strategy that is separate from your corporate and competitive strategies.

2. Consider the following questions to accelerate your progression through the sustainability strategy maturation process:
   - If your company is moving from Stage 1 to Stage 2, have you
     - Conducted a materiality assessment to identify and confirm with stakeholders the most material, sustainability-oriented issues your company must plan for and embrace?
     - Framed sustainability as a lens to identify business risks and opportunities?
     - Appointed a team to be responsible for crafting sustainability strategy?
     - Charged this team with creating alternative scenarios and ideas to develop and document a robust sustainability strategy?
   - If your company is moving from Stage 2 to Stage 3, have you
     - Implanted your highly material issues into your company's corporate and competitive strategic-planning processes?
     - Ensured your corporate culture embraces sustainability thinking? Translated the ethos of sustainability into terms meaningful to your business?
     - Placed accountability for nurturing and executing business unit–level sustainability actions in the hands of the business unit, function, and/ or regional managers as appropriate?

5

LEADING STRATEGY AND MANAGEMENT EFFORTS

In Chapter Four we learned powerful ways to integrate sustainability into corporate and competitive strategies. In this chapter we explore how companies are installing governance structures to oversee their sustainability efforts.

Sustainability Governance at Herman Miller

Herman Miller, an office equipment company perhaps best known for its amazingly comfortable Aeron line of office chairs, has been integrating sustainability into business activities for more than two decades. The story of its formalized sustainability efforts began in 1988. That year, two of its employees crossed paths for the first time. Their chance meeting at a Michigan permit office set in motion the creation of one of industry's oldest environmental sustainability committees: Herman Miller's Environmental Quality Action Team (EQAT).

Paul Murray was one of these employees. Back then, Murray was employed by Herman Miller as a production manager for a new wood-finishing line of products based in Zeeland, Michigan. He had to go to the State of Michigan permitting office to request an air quality permit in support of this new wood finish. In the waiting room, Murray ran into another permit seeker from Herman Miller. The two realized they were seeking similar permits. Shortly after, Murray told this story to a couple of senior Herman Miller officials while jogging. During the jog, Murray and his colleagues decided to approach senior management to create an environmental committee. In 1989 Herman Miller launched the EQAT to develop environmental policies for the company to follow.

The EQAT has grown in stature over the subsequent twenty years. Murray allowed that the ability to change with the times is the secret sauce in EQAT's ongoing success. Herman Miller has realized that new members need to come in as peoples' jobs change. When EQAT first started, the focus was environmental stewardship. Now it's about environmental footprint, health and safety, design for the environment, and other more strategic pursuits. As such, the EQAT has switched people in and out to ensure the collective ability to meet the organization's needs.

The EQAT serves as a critical component of Herman Miller's sustainability governance structure. Herman Miller's board is updated quarterly on the company's sustainability progress; two of the chief executive officer's (CEO) ten performance metrics track sustainability progress. In addition to the EQAT and board-level oversight, sustainability at Herman Miller is also guided by a newly created corporate social responsibility (CSR) committee. Chaired by their CEO, the CSR committee identifies sustainability initiatives for the EQAT and the rest of Herman Miller to deliver.

Sustainable Market Leaders' General Approach to Governance

Sustainable Market Leaders approach sustainability differently than do their peers. Whereas their peers often embrace sustainability via a piecemeal approach, if at all, Sustainable Market Leaders apply an enterprise approach to sustainability. Their more holistic view of sustainability is informed by their belief that sustainability needs to be an integral component of their core strategies.

Four groups of people work together to govern Sustainable Market Leaders' sustainability efforts. (See Figure 5.1.) The first

Figure 5.1 Robust Sustainability Governance Structures

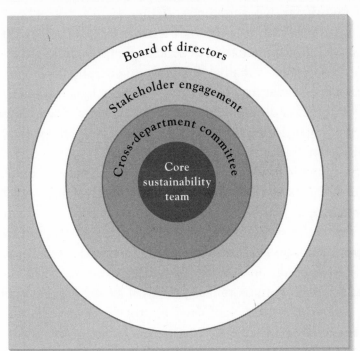

and most responsible for managing sustainability on a daily basis is the core sustainability team. Typically a cross-department committee is responsible for making sustainability strategy decisions. A group of engaged stakeholders, usually a mix of nongovernmental organizations (NGOs), academics, and customers, provides feedback and guidance on sustainability strategy decisions. Ultimately sustainability performance is overseen by either a board subcommittee or the board writ large. I discuss each of these groups in more detail later in this chapter.

To carry out their sustainability visions, Sustainable Market Leaders have installed a core team of sustainability experts. These sustainability professionals are appointed to manage the company's sustainability strategy, progress, and stakeholder interactions. Their efforts inform the company's day-to-day sustainability efforts, which are then overseen and implemented by a sustainability governance structure.

These governance structures include board-level oversight, cross-discipline sustainability councils, and stakeholder advisory groups. Together, sustainability governance structures provide Sustainable Market Leaders with a mixture of fiduciary oversight, silo-busting coordination, and a flow of expertise that is increasing the value Sustainable Market Leaders are harvesting from their sustainability strategies.

Sustainable Market Leaders employ governance structures for at least three reasons. First, equipping their highest levels of governance to provide oversight sends to employees, shareholders, and other stakeholders a powerful signal of the company's commitment to sustainability. For employees, the signal is their company's commitment to sustainability. Armed with this knowledge, employees are more likely to consider the impact a potential course of action will have on the company's pursuit of sustainability. And for shareholders and stakeholders alike, the signal conveys the company's belief that climate change harbors a material risk to the business's ongoing operations.

Second, engaging representatives from each of the company's functions in the design and management of a sustainability strategy provides companies with multiple benefits. Involvement, coming mainly in the form of sustainability councils, provides informal but much needed sustainability knowledge transfer to senior executives. That is, sustainability councils bring together a mixture of experienced sustainability practitioners and senior business leaders in an effort intended to facilitate integration of sustainability into strategy. Beyond knowledge transfer, cross-representation also can help ensure the type of business unit and/or function support that can be the difference between implementation failure and success. Coordination and best practice sharing are also more likely to occur when representatives across the business interact.

Third, developing relationships with NGOs, academics, and other external entities provides companies with society-based listening posts. Sustainable Market Leaders are developing these relationships by inviting their external partners to provide advice, expertise, and brutally honest advice to senior business leaders. Often these exchanges occur during formal stakeholder advisory meetings, which comprise the third part of well-developed sustainability governance structures.

How Widespread Is the Installation of Sustainability Governance Structures?

The installation of robust sustainability governance is one determining factor that separates Sustainable Market Leaders from their less sustainability-sophisticated peers. For clarity, I use the phrase "sustainability governance structures" as a blanket term that includes core sustainability management teams, cross-department sustainability committees, formal stakeholder advisory panels, and board- (or equivalent) level oversight.

Among the 2010 Global Fortune 500 member companies, I found evidence that slightly more than 200 companies (205) have installed a core team of sustainability professionals. Separately, 196 companies have established cross-department sustainability committees to regularly discuss sustainability issues. Nearly 130 have created stakeholder advisory panels from which they receive guidance, advice, and constructive criticism on their sustainability commitments and progress to date. And nearly 40 percent (186 companies) count on their boards to provide sustainability oversight. Of these companies, the majority (116) have either created new board-level sustainability committees or asked current committees to provide sustainability oversight.

As the data suggest, sustainability governance structures are not widespread. But a deeper dive into the numbers reveals that Sustainable Market Leaders account for a disproportionate share

Figure 5.2 Sustainability Governance Structures Among 2010 Global Fortune 500 Companies and Sustainable Market Leaders

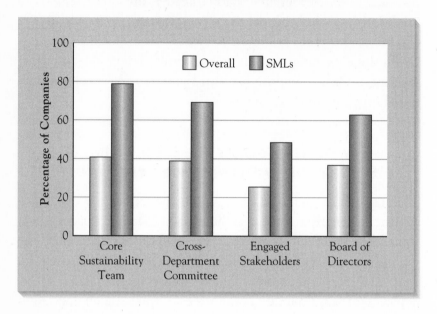

of the total number of Global Fortune 500 companies that employ each of the mentioned vehicles of sustainability governance (see Figure 5.2).

This chapter focuses on the development and deployment of these four components of robust sustainability governance structures. Each section of the chapter helps build the subsequent section as a means to create a holistic picture of governance. The first section is dedicated to those professionals installed as part of their company's central sustainability team. The second section looks at the cross-department committees Sustainable Market Leaders have installed. The third section explores the use of and reliance on stakeholder advisor panels as a means of bringing in external opinions. And the final section is dedicated to the installation of board-level sustainability oversight.

Core Sustainability Team

Most Sustainable Market Leaders have installed a full-time group of employees to spearhead at least the development of their sustainability efforts. In some cases, the group is a centralized team with a name such as the corporate social responsibility department (Air France-KLM) or the sustainability center (BASF). In other cases there are several collaborating teams, each focusing on a specific aspect of sustainability and reporting separately to one or more members of senior management.

While the makeup of Sustainable Market Leaders' sustainability teams differs, the remit of these teams is remarkably similar. In general, Sustainable Market Leaders make their core sustainability teams accountable for proposing policies, providing expertise, managing stakeholder relationships, coordinating sustainability initiatives, sharing best practices, and measuring and reporting progress toward sustainability objectives. Consider the remit of the corporate responsibility (CR) team at GlaxoSmithKline, from the company's website:

> We have a small central CR team to coordinate policy
> development and reporting specifically with respect to CR, and
> to communicate with socially responsible investors and other
> stakeholders.[1]

A growing number of Sustainable Market Leaders have installed a combination of core sustainability teams and regionally located sustainability management teams. Brian Larnerd at Hitachi, for example, oversees Hitachi's global CSR strategy and coordinates regional CSR efforts with colleagues in Japan, China, India, and throughout Europe. These regional sustainability managers are responsible for applying local flavors to global sustainability dicta to ensure the policies are relevant to and in compliance with local norms, customs, and regulations. Typically team calls are held monthly to coordinate efforts and discuss concerns and best practices along the way.

Sustainability neither fits into only one function nor controls a set of finite corporate resources. As a result, core teams focus on *influencing*, not *controlling*, the sustainability direction of their organizations. For example, consider the approach Ben Packard and his global responsibility team employ at Starbucks:

> One of the things our team does is tackle issues we spot on the horizon. Not acute issues that require immediate, emergency attention. For example, what is a green building when you've already laid out the intention that you're a green company? We were searching for a way to define whether our stores were green in a way that gave us outside assurance that they were and also gave our stakeholders the credibility and authenticity to believe that we're doing it right. So my team and I worked with the U.S. Green Building Council. In my role as director of environmental impact at that time, I served as chair of the retail development committee of the U.S. Green Building Council, with close counsel from our global development team. My role was to help inform how the standard was going to be developed.
>
> My team and I have had very little to do with the execution of green buildings within Starbucks. Three years ago we made a commitment once the standard was written that, beginning in December 2010, we were going to build all new, company-owned stores to achieve LEED certification. That has been fully absorbed as the way we do business.
>
> Similarly when human rights and environmental claims were established for how we wanted to buy manufactured goods, my team set the standards and does the benchmarking but our buyers work directly with suppliers. We are overseeing the verifiers that we're using. So my focus at the moment is to further integrate increased performance here because we simply do not have the capacity—it's just not scalable. The global responsibility team does not buy the coffee, doesn't build stores, doesn't select paper choices, nor do we select the

lighting equipment. Instead, we engage, influence, and support all the people who do these essential jobs so that at the end of the day the performance against our responsibility goals is top-notch.

Cross-Department Committees

What if your core sustainability management team recommended a shift from air- to water-borne transport as a means to reduce your environmental footprint? Such a shift would affect multiple functions: transportation and logistics (method of shipping changed), relationship management (product delivery dates will vary), and finance (in transit products will sit on the balance sheet longer). You would probably pull together representatives from each function, perhaps starting with a presentation from the person recommending the switch in mode of transportation. The function executives might resist this change for one or more reasons. "Why should we adjust a system that has worked so well?" "This is the first I'm hearing of this idea." "What is sustainability?"

The vast majority of sustainability initiatives, ranging from materiality assessments to value chain adjustments, require the coordination of efforts across multiple departments. In recognition of the need for such collaboration, more and more Sustainable Market Leaders have installed one or more sustainability working groups. By "sustainability working groups" I mean council, committee, team, or any other term that companies use to describe the group of colleagues brought together to coordinate, formulate, and implement their sustainability strategy.

Surprisingly, despite the varied range of companies that comprise the Global Fortune 500, the form that deployed cross-department committees take does not vary greatly. I reviewed the charters of more than 150 cross-department committees to better understand why and how companies deploy these structures. I reached two conclusions. First, the remit of cross-department committees does not vary greatly by industry or geographic location. Second, the structure of these cross-department committees also does not greatly differ. However, some wrinkles do exist.

Mandates of the Committees. My research benefited from the thoughtful disclosure of sustainability management group charters and structures on companies' websites and/or their responses to the Carbon Disclosure Project's 2009 questionnaire. In most cases, companies provided enough detail about the purpose of their sustainability working groups to offer a flavor of what the groups really do. In brief, these working groups are charged with setting and executing (at a high level) the company's sustainability strategy.

Australia & New Zealand Banking Group's (ANZ Banking Group) sustainability working group, which is called the ANZ Banking Group Corporate Responsibility Committee, includes the following responsibilities:

- Working with ANZ Banking Group's management board to provide strategic leadership of ANZ Banking Group's CR agenda
- Identifying and monitoring current and emerging corporate responsibility risks and opportunities
- Reporting and advising ANZ Banking Group's management board on strategies to respond to these risks and opportunities
- Agreeing on ANZ Banking Group's public corporate responsibility targets and commitments in consultation with the management board
- Integrating corporate responsibility policies and management systems across the business
- Reviewing and approving all significant programs and expenditure relevant to corporate responsibility strategy[2]

Most cross-department sustainability committee remits I studied included responsibility for identifying opportunities and risks (i.e., determining the most important aspects of sustainability pertaining to the company's situation), crafting sustainability strategies, setting sustainability policies, coordinating the execution of these strategies, and renewing the company's sustainability strategy over time.

Typically these committees' purposes and activities are documented by a charter. The committees meet between two and six times per year. For example, the ANZ Banking Group CR committee meets six times per year, but urgent interim business is sometimes handled less formally through proxy decision making.

Structure of the Committees. One of the key purposes of sustainability working groups is to foster collaboration across an enterprise's departments and business groups. This collaboration is critical because responsibility for sustainability does not neatly reside within one function's remit; the sustainability manager needs to use influence, not control, to achieve progress against sustainability objectives.

A broad sampling of Sustainable Market Leaders' working groups suggests the importance of gaining cross-enterprise support to successfully integrating sustainability. For example, ANZ's Corporate Responsibility Committee is chaired by the chief executive officer (CEO). In addition to the CEO, the committee consists of senior leaders from across the company, including

- Group managing director, human resources
- Group managing director, operations, technology, and shared services
- Group managing director, strategy, M&A, marketing, and innovation
- CEO, institutional division
- Group general manager, corporate affairs
- Group general manager, innovation[3]

A separate aspect of sustainability working groups' success is that they rely on subcommittees to provide more concentrated amounts of time on specific sustainability issues. As Paul Murray at Herman Miller explained:

> The EQAT meetings consist of a regular update of the status, to allow for a better discussion to create the goals for the company. Indeed one major component of EQAT is goal and strategy setting for how we're going to get there and what we want to work on. The other part of the meeting is dedicated to an evaluation and consideration of specific programs like energy efficiency. To ensure these important topics receive the needed amount of attention, we've set up several subcommittees, one on energy for example. So the energy subcommittee might say, "Here are the top five things that we want to do for energy efficiency in the next year." Once their analysis is complete, they'll run it by EQAT, to keep EQAT up to speed with, "Here's how we're proceeding to implement the goals and strategy that you have put out there as a company."
>
> Initially we didn't have subcommittees so EQAT had to do both. But with these subcommittees, EQAT meetings are now more focused on report outs from the subcommittee work. In this way, we keep senior executives up to speed so that we're better informed to be able to set the strategy and make changes if we need to and regularly keep track of what we're working on. To get a sense of the impact of the subcommittees, EQAT used to be an all day meeting. In fact, the last EQAT meeting we had, we finished in about an hour and fifteen minutes. That's because we have kept them, or the focus has become more laser-like to what their expectations are. That's one of the main reasons why the subcommittees really work well for us.

Sustainable Market Leaders have come to realize that the composition of executives who participate on the sustainability committee will need to adjust over time as the committee's needs and responsibility evolve. Paul Murray reflected on the ability to change EQAT's composition over time:

> We have three EQAT members that have been part of the team for a very long time. The rest of the EQAT members have flexed in and out. Our most recent flexing has changed the team's composition from low to medium management, to medium to upper, upper being directors. The reason we needed to flex is that when we first started, EQAT was about environmental stewardship only. It has become much more strategic. As such, we needed to flex a little bit more into decision makers at a different level than what we had had in the past. As it became more strategic, we have to be able to think a little bit longer out.

I asked Murray for advice on how to identify the right people to join EQAT:

> You've got to find people that are truly interested in it, as a concept not as a career builder. What I mean by that is that we've had a few people that recognize that, "Hey this is becoming really popular. I'm going to get on it." These folks are well intentioned but they do emails and read their Blackberries through the whole meeting. They're more of a distraction than they are a help. Make sure you get the right partnership. And don't be surprised where you find your volunteers or your champions.

Wrinkles in Remit and Structure. While Sustainable Market Leaders' sustainability committees are remarkably similar in remit and structure, they can differ in other respects. For example, some working groups are much more specific than others about the type and scope of business decisions requiring approval from the working group. For example, ANZ Banking Group's corporate responsibility committee must "review and approve all significant CR programs and expenditure in excess of $250,000."[4]

While most Sustainable Market Leaders have developed some form of cross-department committee, these working groups are not without their drawbacks. The most often cited concern is that working through such a committee lengthens the time required to make sustainability-related decisions. While I agree decision making takes longer when committees are involved, I believe the time invested up front is far less than the time required begging for forgiveness if one makes unilateral sustainability decisions that affect others' areas of responsibility.

Not every company employs a sustainability committee. Some choose not to, based either on experience or intuition. Consider Starbucks. As Ben Packard relayed:

> We do not have a central organizing sustainability committee. We had that for a couple years and moved away from that model. Our sustainability strategy has the benefit of very clear goals and enterprise intention, which are stated at the highest level of our strategic plan. So we do not need a central sustainability committee. To us, that would be redundant.

Stakeholder Engagement

Sustainability requires paying attention to both environmental and social interactions. My review of the Global Fortune 500 shows that companies take two distinct approaches to receiving guidance: feedback and dialogue.

Dialogue with stakeholders comes at a price. Companies must be willing to contribute resources to the cause of NGOs, actively seek honest (and often difficult to hear) feedback from customers, and make available their unvarnished environmental and social inefficiencies to all facets of society. Many companies still suffer from the "folded arm" syndrome: "We're not interested in the gripes of a select few." More and more companies are moving beyond this myopic, and frankly, egotistic point of view, and the dialogues they foster make them agile when they need to be.

Feedback

Most companies simply seek feedback. They request it from society by push and pull, using one or more of three tactics:

1. *An annual survey that solicits feedback on the company's environmental and social performance.* Often these surveys are available on the company's website for a period of time and are open to the general public. Results (or selected portions of them) are usually published in the company's annual sustainability report. Annual surveys can also be distributed to a targeted group of stakeholders. Some companies employ third-party survey vendors to field the survey to certain NGOs, customers, and/or suppliers.
2. *Interviews, either one-on-one or in focus groups.* This tactic is effective for companies seeking direct and unbounded answers to targeted questions aimed at select stakeholders. Occasionally companies will publish snippets of these interactions for all to see.
3. *Requests to the general public for feedback.* This differs from annual surveys in that the request is year-round, open-ended, and unguided (i.e., without multiple choice questions). The most common means of answering these requests is an email address at the end of a company's annual sustainability report, generally with the message "Please tell us how we are doing" or something similar.

Numerous Sustainable Market Leaders successfully use a combination of the three. Consider Bayer, the giant German chemical concern. Via the company's inclusion on the Dow

Jones Sustainability Index, and the FTSE4GOOD Index, among others, Bayer has received its fair share of acclaim for its sustainability program. The company is not content with the status quo; it is seeking feedback from stakeholders as a means to continuous improvement of the sustainability initiative. It uses surveys, interviews, and other means. For example, the company has commissioned a website, www.survey.sustainability.bayer.com, to enable readers of their annual sustainability report to suggest ideas for improvement. In addition, Bayer has included a link to their annual sustainability survey on the portion of their website dedicated to sustainable development. Finally, in preparation for their 2009 annual sustainability report, Bayer conducted 200 phone interviews with representatives from numerous stakeholder groups.[5]

Dialogue

Other companies prefer to foster two-way dialogue at "stakeholder advisory councils," regular recurring meetings. These meetings typically bring together senior managers from the company's business units with representatives from NGOs, academic groups, customers, and the like. Usually these councils meet at least twice a year for frank discussions of the company's progress toward sustainability goals.

Some companies see this approach as a means to head off criticism-laden reports from stakeholders before these reports are published. One industrial equipment company, for example, told me that twice it has been able to hear about a negative draft report being prepared by an NGO via its stakeholder advisory council. The company was able to engage the NGO in honest (and somewhat heated) discussion about the report, corrected some misinformation, and influenced the tone of the report to be more neutral.

Companies as varied as BT, Unilever, HP, Zurich Financial Services, BHP Billiton, BMW, and Sodexo employ such a council.

For example, consider BT's leadership panel. The panel is an advisory group of experts from think tanks, consultancies, government, and industry. The panel meets four times per year to "provide independent guidance and expert advice on key areas of CR (corporate responsibility) strategy and performance." Specific topics covered in 2009, for example, included the development of BT's key CR programs, CR strategy review and governance changes, and BT's materiality review and key performance indicators.

To better understand the thought process behind a company's decision to install a stakeholder engagement panel, consider Sodexo Group's story, as recounted by Arlin Wasserman, the company's vice president of corporate citizenship. Sodexo is the giant food and facilities management company based in Marseille, France, founded by current Chairman Pierre Bellon in 1966. Employing 380,000 people and serving 50 million customers worldwide, it has grown through the acquisition of numerous food service companies over the past four decades. With annual revenues of nearly $20 billion, Sodexo's North American business units account for almost 40 percent of revenue; European business units account for 37 percent. According to Wasserman:

> At Sodexo Group we made the decision that we were going to embark on a strategy that was about transparent, measurable reporting on progress toward specific sustainability goals. We have put together a stakeholder panel of between twelve and sixteen NGOs that span the wide array of our business from nutrition to sustainable food and agriculture, energy management, and facilities management.
>
> The first action for the panel was to codify the materiality areas that we would focus our targets on, and then to go through the process of identifying metrics that mean something. Based on this materiality assessment, we came back to the panel with specific goals. This process has created some tension in our company, which has traditionally been insular—we really

haven't engaged with stakeholders in open dialogue. We've often engaged in listening and telling, but we haven't participated in co-creation and dialogue. So we've gone along that path in North America.

So we're actively building our sustainability goals and the implied roadmap to reach them while we're doing stakeholder engagement. Stakeholder engagement is intended to make sure that when we go public with that next level of detail and the next level of detail after that, we know the hard questions we'll be asked. The panel is making us look at these questions. This exercise will also help us to avoid key mistakes. So part of it is just kind of getting the hardest questions out first. And part of it is also creating that group of people who will stay with us and comment on our reporting as we go. Yes, they're vested in our success, but basically for us it's about having a sounding board. We need this assistance since our company is insular enough that we struggle to see our own faults, or know that there really are best practices. And it's easier for an outside party to sometimes say that than it is the sustainability office.

When globally we decided to develop a sustainability strategy called, "The Better Tomorrow Plan," which closely mirrored what we were already doing in North America, engagement was one of the strategy's three pillars. That is we engage, which is meant to say we are open to dialogue with stakeholder groups about how to do improve our business. What that looks like for our company is not well defined. We've done some internal exercises about what it would be like to have a stakeholder panel and what might we do if they highlighted an area that we need improvement. And we were not comfortable with how that might play out.

At the same time we realized that globally we didn't have the human resources to really address this issue in many of our smaller divisions; my team (Sustainability and Corporate Social Responsibility) couldn't stretch. So in mid-2010 we created our first-ever global partnership with an NGO to provide technical

assistance to us. The World Wildlife Fund is going to help us
with sourcing farm and ranch products and seafood and also
provide management training to help cascade standard practices.
So that's been a big opening for us. In fact we recently had our
global steering committee meeting for sustainability in Paris. We
had three people from WWF attend half our meeting. This is the
first time ever that we had a non-Sodexo executive at the table
involved in decision making.

Choosing NGOs to Engage

How do Sustainable Market Leaders decide with which NGOs
to engage? For insight here I turned to Mark Heintz, currently
the director of sustainability and corporate responsibility at
Deckers Outdoor Corporation. Prior to joining Deckers, Mark
led HP's Stakeholder Relations program. Mark has recently
helped Deckers determine the specific NGOs to approach for
partnerships and support. His experience and insights are consistent with the approaches Sustainable Market Leaders have
pursued over the past few years. In fact, he used the below stakeholder mapping technique at HP. Here's how Heintz approaches
this critical question:

> I use the following three-step prioritization process to identify
> NGOs with which to engage. The first step is to map all
> relevant NGOs on a grid. Along one axis, say the x-axis, is the
> power and influence of the NGO. And then along the y-axis,
> the vertical axis, is the willingness to collaborate with the
> private sector. The ideal organizations would be in the upper
> right quadrant. [See Figure 5.3.]
>
> The next step of that prioritization process is to do a deep
> dive. Look at the NGOs' focus areas. Are they focusing on
> environmental issues or human rights or energy or supply
> chain or whatever? What are their main geographic locations?
> How large is their sphere of influence? Also how business

Figure 5.3 Template for Prioritizing NGOs

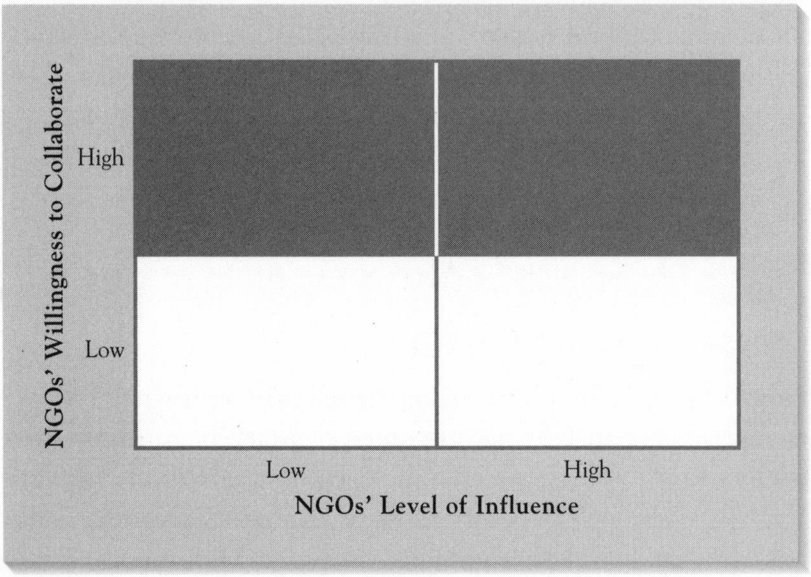

savvy are they? Some NGOs are just more accustomed to working with business than others. Lastly was just to look at the funding sources and motivation and drivers and that perspective.

Board-Level Sustainability Oversight

Formally tasking a company's board to provide oversight of the company's sustainability strategy is the fourth component of Sustainable Market Leaders' sustainability governance structures. Companies give various reasons for engaging the board in the development and management of their sustainability strategy. Some think the board can "see the forest" for, well, the forest. Released from daily tasks, the board can ask the kind of big picture sustainability questions that prevent a company's sustainability strategy from becoming outdated.

Other companies engage the board to lend gravitas to the company's sustainability strategy. After all, boards are required to provide oversight to risk mitigation and compliance efforts; by blending sustainability into this area of oversight, a company can signal its belief that environmental and social dignity is material to its operations to the very stakeholders likely to otherwise pursue shareholder resolutions as a path to getting a company to commit to sustainability.

Another reason to engage the board is that board-level oversight helps keep management honest, a critical determinant of trust and reputation these days. If the board is truly independent and includes highly accomplished, insightful individuals, it should be able to sniff dishonesty from afar. They should be able to get beyond an argument's prima facie case, requiring senior leadership to demand answers from their direct reports in response to the board's probing questions. Such a demand for accountability should lead to the installment of systems, whether technological or policy, that will increase a company's transparency, further inspiring an increased level of trust in the company among stakeholders and other observers.

Opinions differ about the most effective way to task a company board with sustainability oversight. Two options prevail, as shown in Figure 5.4. The first is regularly placing sustainability on the agenda of "full" (that is, general) board meetings. The second is focusing a portion of the board on sustainability, either by creating a new board-level committee focused on sustainability or by blending sustainability oversight into an existing board committee. Each approach presents pros and cons.

Blend Sustainability Oversight into General Board Meetings. One approach to equipping the board to provide sustainability strategy oversight is by including formal sustainability progress reviews during general board meetings. Many companies prefer this approach because it engages the board's entire suite of capabilities and insights. One of the main challenges this approach presents is the limited attention paid to sustainability by a busy board. If five agenda items need to be covered during

Figure 5.4 Two Options for Board-Level Sustainability Oversight

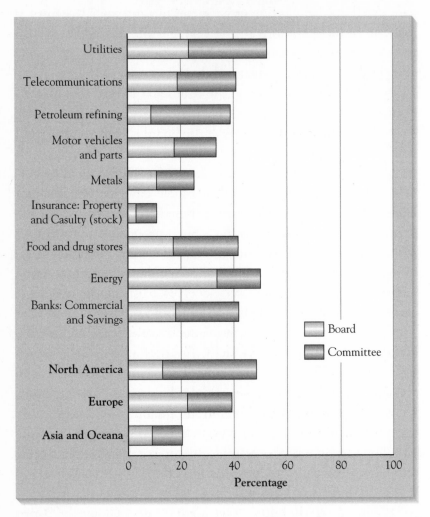

any given board meeting, there's no guarantee sustainability will receive its deserved attention. While fewer than half of the Global Fortune 500 companies with board-level sustainability oversight employ this approach, the companies that do employ this approach find the board's feedback no less timely or insightful.

Brian Walker, Herman Miller's CEO, provides quarterly sustainability updates to his company's board. Two of his ten quarterly performance metrics are sustainability related, providing a platform for the board to both evaluate his company's performance against sustainability goals and provide actionable advice to further refine Herman Miller's sustainability strategies.

Australia & New Zealand Banking Group's board is responsible for reviewing the company's performance against its environmental charter on an annual basis. In addition, the board receives quarterly updates on the company's progress against its sustainability objectives.

In January 2010, Apple's board formally rejected a shareholder petition to establish a separate committee to oversee the company's sustainability efforts. The board noted its belief that it "gets regular reports on the company's environmental initiatives which are making significant progress, so it does not need a dedicated sustainability committee."[6] This event demands additional observation, as the fallout from Apple's shareholder groups, among other stakeholders, might provide clues as to the future (and preferred) vehicle for board-level oversight of a company's sustainability efforts.

Establish a Separate Committee. As shown in Figure 5.4, many companies, including 62 percent of 2010 Global Fortune 500 companies that engage their boards, imbue a committee of the board with oversight responsibility. A review of this subgroup of the 2010 Global Fortune 500 suggests the focused ability to provide advice to the board and the executive management team is the primary reason for this vehicle of choice. In North America, a significantly larger percentage of companies employ a committee than do companies in other regions.

The committees are tasked in part or in full with providing oversight of their company's environmental and social sustainability goals, flaws, and initiatives. Companies choosing this option believe they gain more value from having a portion of their board provide focused guidance on sustainability than from having the full board consider sustainability as part of general board meetings.

The topic is timely: many companies have established their board-level sustainability committees within the past three years. Typically these committees consist of three or four directors and meet quarterly to review the company's sustainability progress, usually presented by either the company's CEO or head of sustainability. If an issue of materiality is discussed and requires full board review, the sustainability committee presents the issue to the full board during the next board meeting.

Companies in this category include Centrica, Glaxo-SmithKline (GSK), HP, 3M, and Nike. GSK's corporate responsibility committee (CRC) provides an illustrating example. According to GSK, the CRC

> meets three times a year to review our policies and progress on our CR Principles. The committee reviews performance against five of CR principles annually. These are access to medicines, standards of ethical conduct, research and innovation, employment practices, and community investment. Other principles are discussed at least once every two years. The committee reports its findings to the board. The committee also reviews and signs off the annual performance information published on the company's website and the company's annual corporate responsibility highlights document.

Weight the Options. I believe sustainability is about both opportunity pursuit and risk mitigation. A disadvantage of housing sustainability oversight in the audit committee or a similar type of committee is that it could limit the board's ability to provide actionable advice that will lead to the kind of growth that investors desire. In addition, sustainability is the kind of "all hands on deck" imperative that benefits from a wide range of top thinkers' advice and guidance.

Ultimately the question of which structure to install comes down to two considerations:

1. *The extent to which sustainability is material to your company's performance.* If your view is that sustainability is material primarily (but not solely) as a risk, then housing sustainability oversight within a risk committee or similar board body makes sense. Doing so ensures sustainability progress will be viewed regularly, by eyes hardened by years of effective risk mitigation efforts. Concerns can then be raised to senior management "off cycle"; that is, senior management does not need to wait until the next formal board meeting to be appraised of the board's concerns.

2. *Your directors' fluency with the topic of sustainability.* A board that has a subset of sustainability-fluent directors might find having a separate committee to be the most effective use of the full board contingent's time. That being said, as sustainability has become a mainstream imperative, more and more directors have become at least conversant with sustainability challenges and opportunities. To wit, according to a recent Deloitte survey of 220 directors of U.S. companies with at least $1 billion in annual revenue, more than three-quarters of respondents claim to have at least a moderate understanding of the business risks and opportunities associated with sustainability.[7]

In addition to the benefit of allocating board time to sustainability risk oversight, establishing a new board committee also appeals to stakeholders. Indeed, more and more sustainability research firms weigh whether a company has established a separate board committee when assessing a company's overall sustainability progress. But setting up a new committee usually requires board approval, places new demands on directors' time, and might result in a filtering of the information about sustainability progress the full contingent of the board hears.

Conclusion

At the risk of understatement, a lot of work is required to form and execute an effective sustainability strategy. Not only do conditions change over time, but conditions differ by region. To be effective, the strategy must at least consider its impact on a range of stakeholders. And, of course, the strategy needs to deliver positive cash flow to receive additional investment. It takes a village to embrace sustainability.

Sustainable Market Leaders are up to the task. Despite the scope, industry, and geographic location differences among them, these companies have installed remarkably similar sustainability governance structures. These commonalities include

- A sustainability team, typically housed within a corporate function that resides outside a business unit
- One or more sustainability working groups that bring together representatives from the company's functions, business units, and regional operations
- Regular recurring stakeholder engagement, either via feedback mechanisms, such as surveys, or ongoing dialogue, in the shape of formalized meetings between stakeholders and executives
- Board level sustainability oversight, dispersed through either a separate board committee or general board meetings

DIAGNOSTIC

Core Sustainability Team

1. Does your company have one or more employees charged with responsibility for spearheading your company's day-to-day efforts to embrace sustainability?

2. Has your company benchmarked the scope of this team's duties not only against peers but also against one or more Sustainability Market Leader's central group of sustainability experts? In what areas does your team compare favorably? Lag?

3. Does your sustainability team have the political capital necessary to work with their function, business unit, and regional colleagues to execute sustainability strategies? At the very least, does your sustainability team interact on a regular basis with their colleagues within your enterprise?

Cross-Department Committee

1. Does your company have at least one formal network of business representatives that meets regularly to discuss sustainability progress and roadblocks?

2. Does your company operate in numerous countries where regulations and stakeholder demands require a local touch?

3. Does the composition and remit of your sustainability working group adjust to reflect the prevalent expectations of senior management? When was the last time your sustainability working group shuffled its membership?

Stakeholder Engagement

1. Would the stakeholders most important to your success say that their advice, feedback, and concerns are well received and considered?

2. Would your company benefit from holding regular face-to-face meetings with a contingent of representatives from the most important stakeholders?

3. Does your competition have a broader and deeper range of societal listening posts in the form of sustainability stakeholder contacts than you do? Do you honestly believe your company is likely to learn about an emerging imperative before your competition?

Board-Level Sustainability Oversight

1. How material to your company's overall success is sustainability? What is your board's level of interest in having a separate committee view sustainability progress in more detail?

2. To what extent does your company regularly update the board on sustainability progress against objectives?

3. Is your full contingent of board directors fluent in sustainability's issues and opportunities?

6

EMBEDDING SUSTAINABILITY INTO THE VALUE CHAIN

In Chapter Five we explored the governance structures Sustainable Market Leaders are installing to oversee their sustainability efforts. In this chapter, we look at the various adjustments Sustainable Market Leaders are making to integrate sustainability into their core processes.

All companies have the basic processes and functions in place to embrace sustainability. Sustainability does not require expensive and disruptive change programs based on new processes. As we will see, these adjustments seem wholly organic extensions of the processes' spirits, if not tasks and activities; none needs to come down on the organization like a sweeping edict from above.

If you suspect that several of the following process adjustments should have been made simply as a general course of good management, I agree with you. The fact that these actions *are* taking place now can either be viewed as an effort specifically to integrate sustainability into core processes, or as an effort to cut costs to survive the roughest recession this generation has seen to date. Perhaps it doesn't matter which.

Sustainability as Catalyst and Source of Agility

For Sustainable Market Leaders, the sustainability movement is catalyzing changes to processes that provide benefits to shareholders and other stakeholders alike. After all, through the lens of sustainability, waste is, well, waste, and sending mountains of used material to landfill through the outdated mentality of cradle-to-grave is but one of waste's many forms. Financial capital can also be wasted. Companies that don't factor an assumption for the price of carbon dioxide (CO_2) emissions when considering proposals to build new hard assets are setting themselves up to be on the short end of "unplanned for" expenses. Goodwill and brand value are also subject to deleterious waste. Companies that neglect training their suppliers on beneficial (and business-building) environmental and social actions are wasting an opportunity to develop goodwill in the local communities that support the suppliers' operations. And brand value is both eroded through accusations of greenwashing and not enhanced through the missed opportunities stemming from not conveying your company's proven sustainability actions to institutional buyers.

And how does agility enter the picture? How does overlaying an additional consideration onto processes make a company more agile? Won't additional complexity slow down decision making? Companies that have installed robust sustainability governance structures are likely to be the same companies that choose to integrate sustainability into core processes. The governance structure provides the sensing capability companies need to be more agile. The process adjustments described in this chapter provide the means for companies to respond to the flow of information from their internal and external networks. If society's voice rises to a level that deeply influences investors' investment decisions or consumers' purchase decisions, these companies will be able to move more fluidly toward more environmentally and/or socially admirable activities.

The key is to see that integrating sustainability into core processes is an extension of *customer-centricity*. In addition to serving institutional and/or individual customers, companies are discovering the benefits of creating value for additional stakeholders, such as the local communities in which they operate. By considering the needs of an expanded set of stakeholders, process owners are building the routines that will come in handy when the next society-driven imperative emerges. Developing this institutional memory now will reduce the number of learning curves Sustainable Market Leaders will need to traverse when the next imperative emerges. Instead of climbing two learning curves—who are the key constituents sparking change and what does the company need to do to respond to the change—Sustainable Market Leaders will be able to focus on the response learning curve. By comparison, the companies that don't develop this institutional memory now will need to move up two learning curves: the imperative's ins and outs and the process routines necessary to create new value for the stakeholders who sparked the imperative.

Five Functions to Retool

The following sections describe how Sustainable Market Leaders are retooling their beliefs and their value chain activities to embrace sustainability. The extent to which corporate culture adopts sustainability will determine how effective functional adjustments will be. With this in mind, I start the discussion by exploring how Sustainable Market Leaders adjust their corporate culture. Then we look at the five functions that need to be retooled and the actions Sustainable Market Leaders are taking to do so:

1. Innovation
2. Talent management
3. Finance
4. Business development
5. Procurement and supply chain management

In the interest of brevity, I have not detailed manufacturing, resource, and energy management process adjustments that are already under way at a large number of companies. Companies have put policies in place that publicly communicate and privately govern the expectations they have placed on their own operations' consumption of paper, water, energy, and other finite commodities. Nor do I cover so-called design for environment policies that govern the integration of environmental sustainability concerns into the product development process. These adjustments are well documented in books such as McDonough and Braungart's *Cradle to Cradle* and are too numerous to describe in the detail they deserve.

Corporate Culture

Every company has one or more stories about times in its history when a well-intended initiative failed, perhaps spectacularly. If you press for a reason why the initiative failed, you'll likely hear about things like "It was ill conceived" or "The timing wasn't right." But inject a dose of truth serum, and more times than not, the real answer will emerge: "The idea wasn't well connected with our culture." Often this is a coded condemnation of a senior management team that was stuck in its ways, insular, and victim of the insidious disease of groupthink. If this situation resonates with the reader's struggles to gain momentum to embrace sustainability, this section provides hope.

"Folded-Arm Syndrome." One challenge common among even the best of Sustainable Market Leaders is what I've come to call the "folded-arm syndrome." Those at the top are fervently disinterested in engaging in an honest dialogue with stakeholders, including employees who are personally passionate about connecting their personal sustainability interests with their company's resources and capabilities.

Consider United Parcel Service (UPS). A privately held company for ninety-two years, UPS succeeded on its ability to continuously improve and carry out incremental innovations. As one person noted, the company had become "very insular." But, as Lynnette McIntire, UPS's director of corporate reputation management, noted, UPS's culture needed to change when the company went public in 1999:

> Everything changed when we decided to be a public company. Now we couldn't just talk to ourselves anymore, we had to talk to other people and we had to get feedback. That was the start to our cultural changes.

Becoming a public company meant operating more transparently. The torrent of environmental and social sustainability surveys led to an epiphany. As McIntire recalled:

> Increasingly over the past few years we were asked a lot of questions about sustainability through formal surveys. We recognized that we were being judged more and more by assessor groups such as the scorecards from Dow Jones Sustainability Index, FTSE4GOOD, Carbon Disclosure project, investor research groups, and NGOs [nongovernmental organizations].
>
>   We didn't have a structure in place to systematically answer these questions. We'd answer these queries in a one-off, uncoordinated manner. As a result we were receiving really bad scores on some of those scorecards. We couldn't understand it because we knew that we were doing everything we were supposed to be doing. Why didn't they get it? Well the reason was is because we weren't approaching the opportunity to fill out those surveys in a systematic way.

The company's understanding about the value of operating transparently led to the creation of a new external communication process. Again McIntire:

> So we created an awards and surveys committee. We tapped into our working committee structure, so if there was a question

about environmental affairs, we would use the working committee to get that information. If it was about our workforce and safety records, we would pull in the people in the committee who were part of that to be the point people to get that data for us. We started to streamline and standardize the language and the numbers. We put up points of accountability and responsibility to fill those out.

Also what they told us is they couldn't easily find the information. We weren't doing a very good job of making things easy for them, both in terms of the sustainability report process, but also in terms of how we presented things on the web so people could find some of that information. We started to take the Global Reporting Initiative seriously and to really build that out and to answer that effectively.

In the process, UPS's culture began to embrace dialogue. As McIntire explained:

We have a lot of pride at UPS. We think we're number one. We will always think we're number one, especially in this area. When we would get a D on something it was just like a killer. From the plaza which is where all the senior managers are, there would come down into this PR department, "Well why did we get a D? How dare they? What's wrong with them?" So then we started talking to all these groups. We started having conversations. "Well, why did you give us this D? We don't think that's right."

The key to UPS's cultural change was that the company remembered its desire to be the best in its business. It adopted a view that external dialogue was another information source that could in turn enable UPS to remain the best at what it does. McIntire:

We started to engage these organizations. And they would respond with variations of "Well, we couldn't find information on the website about this. Or the only thing we could find was some negative article somewhere." We started to benchmark ourselves and we would say, "Well, you know what? We really need to make some changes on this. We really need to address this issue." And again, the working committee gave us a channel to do that, to say to the working committee and then ultimately to the steering committee, "Well, you know what? We've been approached by the Human Rights Campaign and they say that we don't have this, this and this. We really need to do this. We really need to figure out why we don't have this or is it just we haven't thought about it before? And okay, so we need to address that." So we initially used those assessments and those surveys as benchmarks and change agents.

And so then it got comfortable for us to talk to these groups about who we are and what we were doing. It created that first experience with listening to outside groups that we wouldn't in our normal course of conversations have any contact with them. So that was kind of the first phase.

In this new world of sustainability, stakeholders are asking you questions that you don't think are important to you but actually now they are important. We get a lot of environmental questions and procurement requirements, supplier requirements now from Europe that wouldn't be on our radar ten years ago. Trying to address all these issues forced us to say, "Well, we hadn't thought about that. We really need to think about that."

Well, how does that affect us? And then you get into risk mitigation of, "Well, this thing that they're talking about, is that going to be something that could affect us in the long run?" Well, we really need to think that through. So it's innovation, it's risk mitigation, it's being globally responsible. It's using third parties to both make us more credible but also to make us more self-aware on everything and not just environmental things.

Lack of Apparent Connection Between Sustainability and the Drivers of Value Creation. Often the cultural problem simply boils down to a lack of common language between sustainability management and department management. Ben Packard at Starbucks understood this challenge well. He worked and worked at ensuring his sustainability messages were couched in the language of business performance as a means to encourage sustainability adoption among his colleagues:

> We used to refer to our Global Responsibility efforts as "corporate social responsibility" [CSR]. When we went through our transformation two years ago, we redid everything. Seeing our business declining, really changing the way we were going to grow and with our chairman's return as CEO, asking ourselves all the hard questions that maybe some of the growth had covered up.
>
> And one of the things was that CSR was not the language of our culture. CSR was a signal that we were paying too much attention to the trade of CSR and not enough attention to our key stakeholders. Responsibility is core to our own commitment to our customers and our own commitment to each other as employees, who we call "partners." So there was a very deliberate net language change. We simplified what our function does. It's about establishing the responsible business practices for the company, a description that is consistent with our culture.

Innovation

This section details how Sustainable Market Leaders are integrating sustainability into their innovation efforts. To achieve a state of sustainability, we will need more solutions than we currently have. Sustainable Market Leaders understand this; indeed, this simplistic view screams *"Opportunity!"* to these companies.

In response, Sustainable Market Leaders are carefully thinking about how best to source ideas to pursue. My study revealed four main approaches:

1. Adjust existing processes
2. Participate in open sustainability idea exchanges
3. Crowdsourcing

Adjust Existing Processes. Sustainable Market Leaders are developing a pipeline of ideas to bring their sustainability ambitions to life. Critical to their success has been a series of modifications to their innovation processes. First is the idea that every innovation needs to be aligned with the company's sustainability goals.

Consider the disguised story of a consumer packaged goods company that launched a new product package. The package was brilliant; wrapped with a synthetic material, the package literally sparkled when viewed from certain angles. Shortly after launch the company discovered that the new material made the package unrecyclable. The company pulled the product from retailers' shelves, redesigned the package, and relaunched the product. Upon review this company realized that a "stage gate" that confirmed every idea would be beneficial to the company's sustainability goals. Today every innovation idea requires proof that it will add to the company's sustainability performance.

Several companies confidentially shared that they have adjusted the criteria their investment committees use when evaluating whether to fund the exploration of a new idea. There was a time when every idea needed to demonstrate a certain minimal level of return on investment (ROI). If an idea didn't, then unless it had the blessing of a very senior executive, the idea wouldn't receive funding.

The problem with sustainability investments is the difficulty in forecasting returns above a company's internal "hurdle rate": the minimal return on investment needed to receive funding. Sustainable Market Leaders have adjusted how their investment committees make investment decisions. If an idea can clearly demonstrate a significant contribution to their sustainability goals *and* has a positive (I've heard above 10–15 percent) forecast return on investment, even if that return is lower than the company's hurdle rate then the idea will receive funding.

A few companies have gone even farther. They have added one or more stakeholder representatives, usually from nongovernmental organizations with which they partner, to the investment committee. A proposal requires the approval of this representative in order to receive funding.

Participate in Open Sustainability Idea Exchanges. Sustainable Market Leaders like Nike are engaging with peers and non-peers alike to find solutions that will lead to sustainability. The concept of *open innovation* was introduced by Henry Chesbrough, a professor and executive director at the Center for Open Innovation at University of California, Berkeley, in his book *Open Innovation*. Dr. Chesbrough describes open innovation as "The use of purposive inflows and outflows of knowledge to accelerate internal innovation, and expand the markets for external use of innovation, respectively. [This paradigm] assumes that firms can and should use external ideas as well as internal ideas, and internal and external paths to market, as they look to advance their technology."[1,2]

The concept of open innovation is being applied by Sustainable Market Leaders to fuel their pursuit of sustainability. For example, Nike, along with Best Buy and eight other organizations (Creative Commons, IDEO, Mountain Equipment Co-op, nGenera, Outdoor Industry Association, salesforce.com, 2degrees, and Yahoo) launched the GreenXchange in early 2010 to "bring together companies, people, and ideas to create sustainable change that affects us all."[3] These companies are sharing ideas, insights, and patents to help one another solve large challenges to their sustainability goals.

Crowdsourcing. Sustainable Market Leaders are also turning to *crowdsourcing* for ideas and potential solutions to their sustainability challenges. Much like the concept behind open innovation, crowdsourcing is the act of posing a question to the general public, usually via social media, in the hope that someone, somewhere can provide an idea that could lead to a solution to a typically intractable problem.

During my research I looked at three recent crowdsourcing efforts: a leading European retailer's green customer foray, GE's Smart Grid challenge, and eBay's Green Team (discussed in more detail in Chapter Eight).

In 2010 one of Europe's leading retailers launched an online campaign that sought ideas from its customers as to how the company could further its sustainability efforts. I spoke with the company's sustainability leader under the condition of anonymity to learn how the drive for ideas went. She noted that "the response rate was higher than expected, but the ideas were either generic or impractical." A sampling of the ideas included "Use less energy," "Recycle more," and "Eliminate packaging." They have since closed the campaign with minimal to-dos stemming from the campaign.

Compare the retailer's experience with crowdsourcing efforts at GE and eBay. GE launched the "GE ecomagination Challenge: Powering the Grid" in July 2010 with much fanfare. After all, the company, along with four prominent venture capital firms, put up $200 million to fund ideas from society writ large to accelerate the development and adoption of a smart grid. GE created a new website for the effort (www.ecomagination.com), incorporated aspects of social media, and installed a committee to decide which ideas to fund. Between July 13 and September 30, 2010, nearly 4,000 ideas were submitted; collectively these ideas garnered more than 70,000 comments from nearly 70,000 registered users. Every idea was publicly available to both review and support. Jeff Immelt publicly announced the winners of the challenge on December 2, 2010.

Like GE, eBay created a program (Green Team) and website (http://www.ebaygreenteam.com) to tap into the wisdom of crowds. The program's mission is to "inspire the world to buy, sell and think green every day." To date, more than 300,000 sellers—individuals who sell goods on eBay's platform—have signed up to share ideas and views aimed at making eBay a greener sales partner. The eBay Box, a corrugated cardboard box designed to be durable enough to be used by sellers over and over again, is among the ideas that came from this community and have been rolled out.

In the process I discovered three "rules" that companies considering crowdsourcing of sustainability ideas should employ:

1. *Be painfully clear about the results you want from your campaign.* The European retailer's campaign fell flat in part because it wanted basic ideas. While they might not have explicitly said that, they didn't provide any rules of substance to guide their participants' thinking. GE clearly indicated the three categories of ideas they sought (ideas for Renewable Energy, Grid Efficiency, EcoHomes/EcoBuildings). These guidelines served a dual purpose: they led to self-selection of respondents (you're less likely to respond to a smart grid call for ideas if you aren't versed in the smart grid) and they directed respondents to submit best thinking in a focused area.

2. *Embrace transparency.* Transparency helps promote trust—it's easy to trust someone who doesn't have anything to hide. If your company runs a campaign but doesn't publicly display the results, then (potential) participants are left to draw one of three conclusions. Your company (a) didn't receive any ideas, (b) isn't paying enough attention to the

"what should we do after we receive ideas," or (c) doesn't believe the ideas received are good enough to be published. In each of these three scenarios, the observer is less likely to participate. To nurture dialogue among participants and embrace transparency, GE and eBay created websites to document the ideas submitted by participants.

3. *Link the campaign to co-value creation.* GE and eBay implicitly demonstrated their belief that participants' time is valuable. They did this by asking participants to contribute their best thinking to create initiatives that can not only enhance the company's financial and sustainability performance but also enhance an aspect of participants' lives. In GE's case respondents had the opportunity to pitch ideas in return for funding to pursue those ideas. And in eBay's case sellers were asked for ideas that would help grow their businesses in a sustainable manner—a classic example of aligning eBay's sellers' interests with the company's interests.

Crowdsourcing sustainability ideas through social media is a low-risk, low-cost tactic to enhance sustainability performance. By following these three rules, companies will increase the likelihood of a successful crowdsourcing campaign.

Talent Management

Employees, as a group, represent a microcosm of society. This slice of society can provide your company with real-time feedback and advice about society's likely reaction to your company's current and planned sustainability efforts. Employees, individually, are passionate about sustainability and seeking ways to amplify their efforts to better the environment and society by working with your company's resources.

One step is to help employees understand how to act in a manner consistent with sustainability, without simply giving employees a range of "do's and don'ts." In Chapter Four, I described Australia & New Zealand Banking Group's development of a new corporate responsibility (CR) framework. The choice of the word *framework* instead of *strategy* was deliberate. Julie Bisinella explained:

> We call it a framework rather than a strategy. We have a group-wide business strategy and our CR framework has been developed to support that. We looked at the economic, social, and development issues facing the countries where we're operating and identified consistent themes where we as a bank can make a meaningful contribution in the way we run our business. This supports the goal set out by our CEO that wherever we operate, our customers and stakeholders will know what ANZ stands for.
>
> The framework also gives local countries the flexibility to say, "Well, building urban sustainability is not our number one priority here at this particular point in time. What we need to do is focus on building financial capability amongst these particular groups." So there's consistency but there's also flexibility for people, local country managers, local teams to decide, "Well, which of these issues are we going to pursue?"
>
> To that end we will probably only have, at a group level, one or two, three maximum, projects or initiatives that we incubate for the group. But our entire goal any time we're developing and incubating approaches is to do it in such a way that a transition to business ownership is built in to the project timeframe. It's not in any way sustainable to have initiatives run out of a head office department that's called corporate responsibility. If you want CR or sustainability to work for your business, you need to have business managers that are engaged and thinking about these issues as part of their day-to-day role.

Jean Sweeney at 3M described her company's broad efforts to educate employees on sustainability:

Over the last three years we've specifically focused on increasing employee understanding and awareness of sustainability. In the first step, we developed our sustainability principles. Next we increased employee awareness, including implementing a speaker series for employee engagement education. We enlist internal and external presenters to speak monthly about different aspects of sustainability, including corporate governance, climate change, energy, childhood education, recycling, green chemistry, and business strategy.

We choose a broad range of topics to show that sustainability isn't just about environmental concerns. It has a social and economic aspect, too. I often say to employees in these sessions that sustainability is really about everything that a company needs to do to be sustainable in the long term.

We have been running a sustainability newsletter, along with other communication tools, for several years. While we issue the newsletter at our corporate level, some of the businesses actually issue their own e-newsletters that focus on sustainability in their markets. We also recently developed a set of training modules for our salespeople, because they are facing customers each day and need to be able to explain our sustainability practice.

We produced a series of video modules for the sales force which is available to them online. The first module is an overview of the 3M sustainability story including our history around our Pollution Prevention Pays program. There is a module covering how to talk with customers about the environmental and social attributes of a 3M product. Another module covers emerging market trends around sustainability to help them ask questions of the customer about how these trends are affecting them. We focus on a variety of other key topics including climate change and environmental marketing claims.

Finance

Companies integrating sustainability into their finance processes are focusing on four main areas:

1. Investment proposal considerations
2. Pricing strategy
3. Assessing financial/environmental impact tradeoffs
4. Performance management

Investment Proposal Considerations. For many companies, the forecast return on investment of proposed sustainability initiatives is lower than the ROI of competing, nonsustainability-oriented investments. For years the default setting at most companies has been "the proposal with the highest likely ROI wins." Several Sustainable Market Leaders have modified their investment proposal consideration process to evaluate sustainability-oriented proposals more holistically than simply whether these proposals forecast the highest ROIs. Several companies have "green-lighted" certain sustainability-oriented proposals as long as these proposals forecast an environmental impact reduction aspect as well as a positive return on investment.

Pricing Strategy. When I was in business school, I enjoyed reading Eliyahu Goldratt's *The Goal.*[4] The book is a favorite of mine because it made a complex pricing tactic, activity-based costing, accessible by couching the topic within a fiction story. Activity-based costing, in brief, calculates a per-unit cost of each activity that comprises a particular task as a way of developing a price for the unit that provides a positive contribution margin.

I often wonder why industry hasn't ascribed a per unit cost of carbon to each activity, in essence implementing a "green" activity-based costing model. I understand that conducting life cycle assessments are costly and resource intensive. But I wonder if industry will reach a point where the cost of environmental impact (or environmental impact avoidance) will not only factor into prices but also will be required by retailers or customers to be listed alongside the economic price of the product.

I believe companies that have proactively reduced their carbon footprint to levels much lower than their peers have an opportunity (perhaps even an obligation to their shareholders) to leverage this lower-carbon emission profile into a lowest-price strategy. In other words, if your company employs approaches to emit lower carbon per product unit than peers, consider "baking-in" the carbon cost into your product pricing in such a way that you force your competition to publicly acknowledge to consumers that they are laggards in competing on environmental impact.

I have yet to come across an example of a company pursuing such a pricing strategy. But I wonder if we are *that* far away from a point at which lower carbon footprints can translate into competitive pricing strategies.

Assessing Financial/Environmental Impact Tradeoffs. Some companies are putting a slightly different spin on how they integrate sustainability into finance mechanisms: they use sustainability as a lens through which they evaluate logistics tradeoffs. One such tradeoff is whether to transport finished goods across continents via air or water. Air shipping is more expensive, but faster. This method provides companies the benefit of getting products in transit off their balance sheet faster than water. But air freight also emits more carbon than waterborne shipping. At least one Sustainable Market Leader, who has asked to remain anonymous, is currently assessing the impact of such a shift on the balance sheet, customer relationships, and sustainability objectives.

The story of Maersk, the Danish shipping giant, offers a slight variation on this tradeoff analysis. By reducing its top cruising speed by half, the company has cut fuel consumption and carbon emissions by about 30 percent.[5] This practice, in place since 2008, has resonated with some corporate customers concerned with reducing the level of their Scope 3 carbon emissions (CO_2 emitted by their suppliers' actions, as defined by the WBCSD/WRI GHG Protocol). One selling point Maersk is using: it claims its "Super Slow Steaming" service can reduce a customer's whole annual supply chain carbon footprint by 13 percent.[6]

While Maersk has increased its capital costs due to the need to purchase a couple of additional vessels to "maintain the weekly schedule," the company has readily embraced this additional financial investment in order to achieve its sustainability objectives.[7]

Evaluating such financial and environmental tradeoffs as given in the logistics example may enable vendors to implement a variable pricing scheme. I can see a scenario in which customers who want their product as quickly as possible can elect to pay a premium that covers the carbon tax that the vendor will incur via airfreight. Similarly, customers who are more flexible on the timing of receiving goods via Maersk and other shippers' slowest waterborne speeds might be charged significantly less than customers electing the fastest waterborne speeds.

Performance Management. Most Global Fortune 500 companies have made multiyear carbon emissions reduction goals the foundation of their sustainability commitments. To manage their daily sustainability efforts to achieve these commitments, most of these companies have installed a series of key performance indicators (KPIs) that track and measure their environmental and social sustainability progress. The management of these KPIs tends to fall within the remit of the sustainability group, although I suspect sustainability KPI management will eventually be placed within the finance function.

I focus in this section on one emerging sustainability performance management tool that intrinsically connects the finance function with a company's business unit performance: annual carbon emission budgets.

A growing number of companies are installing annual carbon budgets, per business unit, to manage their efforts to achieve their carbon reduction objectives. National Grid, the UK-based utility with operations in the United States, has set a goal to reduce carbon emissions by 45 percent by 2020. The company understands that achieving this goal will require efforts to reduce emissions every day; there isn't a silver bullet to achieve a goal like this. To integrate emission reduction activity into daily business activities, National Grid has installed annual carbon budgets for each of its business units.

Each business group is measured by three targets:

1. Tonnage, which varies by business unit
2. An efficiency target, which divides tonnage by the amount of electricity produced
3. The establishment of a planning process to establish low-carbon emissions in the future

Executives are expected to reduce their group's carbon budget 1 1/2 percent each year until 2050.[8] A portion of the compensation for each business unit's lead, and the company's CEO, is tied to the unit's (and the company's) ability to manage its annual carbon emissions below its budgeted amount for the year.

Business Development

Should established brands communicate a social message, and if so, what should that message be? How can companies promote the sustainability advantages of their products in a way that avoids accusations of greenwashing? How should a company equip its sales force to communicate its products' sustainability advantages to procurement executives? Sustainable Market Leaders don't have all the answers to these brand, marketing, and sales-tactic questions, but their recent actions provide hints for other companies seeking to integrate sustainability considerations into marketing efforts.

Brand Management. Sustainable Market Leaders are adopting the view that their portfolio of brands can have a powerful impact both on society's ability to achieve a state of sustainability and on society's perception of these companies. Many product brands at Global Fortune 500 companies individually are at least as large as entire midsized companies. Understanding these brands' environmental, social, and economic impacts can only help their companies develop a better understanding of their sustainability impacts at the enterprise level.

But to unlock the real power of such understanding requires companies to adopt the view that sustainability can lead to growth through innovation. Consider Unilever. In 2005, the company set out to understand how each of its brands affected people and the environment in the areas where they are sourced, produced, distributed, and used. The company installed a process they eventually dubbed the "Brand Imprint" program to redefine brand value to include an understanding of the impact of brands such as Lipton, Axe, and others on socioeconomic development and sustainability.

For each of its brands, the company assigned a multidisciplinary team to conduct a detailed assessment of the direct and indirect impacts of its products throughout their value chains. The team then gathered insights about the external influences on the brand's future growth, drawing from consumer and stakeholder research. These insights helped the company develop clearer pictures not only of how its consumers have come to rely on these products but also opportunities to help consumers reduce their individual footprints. Armed with these insights, the company's cadre of brand managers has been better equipped to make valuable ties among consumer interests, product function-ality, and marketing messages.

Ambidextrous Marketing: Reserved on the Outside, Vociferous on the Inside. In the fall of 2008 Lexus ran a set of snazzy print ads for the Lexus RX400h, positioning their hybrid SUV as being "perfect for today's environment (and tomor-row's). . . . Driving the world's first luxury hybrid SUV makes environmental, and economic, sense." After receiving several complaints about the ad's green claims, Britain's Advertising Standards Authority (ASA) banned the ads. Similar claims have led the Federal Trade Commission (FTC) to ban ads in the United States. For example, in June 2009 the FTC filed suit against several companies for making "false and unsubstantiated claims that their products were biodegradable."

For years, companies have been accused of greenwashing and similarly misleading advertising. Numerous interviewees con-fided that their company is purposely conservative with its green marketing messages, in large part to avoid such accusations. But silence isn't an effective competitive strategy either. External marketing campaigns provide marketing messages for sales exec-utives to use during sales calls.

For example, a Sustainable Market Leader held an off-site with the sales force dedicated to one of its key accounts. It invited executives from the key account to present ways the company could increase sales through the account. Nestled among the usual suspects like "Lower prices" was "Prove that you are a sustainability leader."

The company was surprised, not because it doubted green features were helpful to sales; rather because it received frequent external recognition for its progressive sustainability actions. This key account's advice suggested that the company was not effectively communicating its sustainability leadership position throughout the company's organization in a way that resonated with its sales force.

Knowing that the global community actively watches its advertising to detect signs of greenwash, especially promotions targeting the individual consumer market, this company has adopted a conservative approach to marketing. The feedback suggested the company needed to find a way to preserve its external modesty while ramping up the sustainability dialogue internally. The company has since developed green marketing engagement strategies for each of its key accounts.

This story should serve as a wake-up call for all companies that serve both individual and institutional customers and are embracing sustainability. Your company might be sacrificing growth opportunities in the institutional market for the sake of limiting the risk of greenwash accusation.

So how can companies simultaneously be "quiet on the outside, and loud on the inside"? Sustainable Market Leaders employ these five steps:

1. *Ensure that the latest events in the greenwash arena inform the design, launch, and execution of your green marketing campaign.* One approach is to develop and maintain a database of greenwash infractions, as noted by the FTC and/or the ASA. Then add a "checkbox" step to the campaign design process that must be met before a proposed new campaign receives approval and funding.

2. *Vet advertising campaigns with internal and external observers before launch.* Since the FTC doesn't prescreen ads for greenwashing claims, companies should consider forming an internal marketing governance committee and leverage their NGO partnerships to cast a skeptical eye toward new campaigns.

3. *Prime consumers to connect with your green campaign.* Companies are employing one or more of the following three approaches to achieve this. Some are communicating their green qualities through visible clues, such as minimal

packaging. Others are working with their industry peers to develop standard eco labels. And various companies are connecting with green product devotees through social media.

4. *Step up efforts to communicate green selling points to your sales force.* Companies in industries as diverse as financial services and high tech are holding teach-ins, seminars, and other events to raise their sales teams' knowledge of their company's green efforts. They're supporting these efforts by producing sales collateral that explains their green messages in terms that are meaningful, not ethereal, to their sales force.

5. *Develop targeted key account environmental sustainability marketing messages that clearly map your green efforts to your key accounts' green focal points.* More and more companies are mapping out each of their key account's green efforts to develop specific engagement strategies.

Procurement and Supply Chain Management

Over the years, numerous companies have lost goodwill with society by the indecent actions of a direct or even indirect supplier. In response, most Global Fortune 500 companies have taken steps to mitigate their risk of exposure to the adverse impact of suppliers' indecent activities. The enactment of sustainable procurement policies and a supplier code of conduct are among the steps many companies have taken.

Sustainable Market Leaders believe there are many reasons to integrate sustainability into their supply chain management processes. Specifically, these companies see supply chain management as ways to mitigate "guilt by association" and to provide value to the local communities in which they operate. Their actions include employing a more diverse set of suppliers than many of their peers, reducing their suppliers' burden of proving compliance with their codes, and providing training to enhance business performance.

Sustainable Procurement Policies and Procedures. More and more companies are integrating sustainability considerations into their procurement processes. In an effort to achieve their environmental and social sustainability commitments, Sustainable Market Leaders are pursuing three actions to integrate sustainability with procurement:

1. *Employing a diverse set of suppliers,* including suppliers owned by women and/or minorities as well as smaller suppliers. For some companies, diversifying their portfolios of suppliers is a means to meet the community development interests of their customers; for others, supplier diversification is a means to meet their own local community interests.

2. *Assigning a specific percentage of a company's vendor of choice decisions to vendors' sustainability progress.* Aviva, the United Kingdom's largest insurance group, assigns a CSR weighting of a minimum 10 percent in its final decision-making process.[9] Most every Sustainable Market Leader is less specific about the weighting of sustainability responses in their tenders, but no less serious about their determination to assess vendor proposals against a set of sustainability principles they developed, with assistance from their sustainability peers.

3. *Equipping their procurement employees to spearhead the modifications through education focused on the issues and opportunities of sustainability.* New regulations, coupled with stakeholders' emerging demands, will drive sustainability to evolve over time. Sustainable Market Leaders have already recognized the importance of modifying their sustainable

procurement rules to remain aligned with sustainability's coming evolutions.

Supply Chain Management. Concerned about the risk of environmental or social indignities arising from their suppliers' daily activities, numerous companies have enacted supplier codes of conduct. These codes spell out the environmental and social behaviors suppliers must continuously exhibit to remain in good stead with the company purchasing their services. Some companies, such as Maersk, are basing supplier conduct codes on the UN Global Compact; others are enacting codes to govern the activities of their owned operations.

To push governance deeper into supply chains, some companies are beginning to require their suppliers to abide by the same code of conduct. BMW, for example, revised its procurement principles in the fall of 2009 "to require tier-two suppliers to adhere to the same social and ecological standards as the tier-one supplier."[10]

More and more companies are regularly assessing whether their suppliers comply with the principles described in their codes of conduct. Often the first step in these assessments is sending a self-assessment form to each supplier in a company's supply chain. These forms serve as an initial line of defense for the purchasing company. The company gathers the responses to a host of environmental and social questions, scans for obvious red flags, and then aggregates all of their supplier responses to scan for systemwide red flags. If a red flag is discovered, the company notifies the supplier and requests an action plan to address the concern.

Some companies make sustainability experts available to suppliers to support remediation efforts. Consider Veolia Environment, a leading waste management and environmental services firm. Veolia's water division gives its suppliers access to twelve sustainability experts to help them plan improvement.[11]

Volkswagen provides a slightly different example of supplier support. The company has established "a contact point for sustainability" within the company who is available to help suppliers address environmental or social challenges in order to comply with Volkswagen's code of conduct. As needed, Volkswagen is also willing to put together an ad hoc expert team consisting of representatives from "environmental protection, human resources, health and safety, purchasing as well as quality assurance."[12]

Suppliers struggle to find the time to fill out self-assessment forms. Imagine filling out a dozen assessments annually, many of which seek similar, but not exactly the same, performance data. For thinly staffed suppliers, proving their compliance with sustainability policies can be financially taxing. With this in mind, a small but growing number of companies are subscribing to third-party data repositories that collect and aggregate suppliers' sustainability performance data. Several Sustainable Market Leaders are leading the way in adopting this approach as a suitable first line of supplier assessment. For example, multiple companies have joined the Suppliers Ethical Data Exchange (SEDEX). SEDEX serves as a repository for suppliers' self-assessments online. SEDEX subscribers can access these self-assessments, eliminating the duplication of reporting separately to each.

Numerous companies are fortifying their oversight of suppliers with the highest risk profiles with formal, in-person audits. Typically, audits are announced in advance and consist of factory and worker dormitory walkthroughs, interviews with management and randomly chosen workers, and feedback meetings aimed at helping the supplier improve their overall performance. For privacy purposes, companies share their findings with the supplier being audited but do not publicly publish the detailed findings.

Given the size and geographic spread of their portfolio of suppliers, many companies use a combination of employees and third-party certified auditors to conduct these onsite supplier assessments. Usually suppliers that serve multiple companies in the same industry will be audited by a third party, with the audit and subsequent findings communicated to all interested purchasers. This approach serves to reduce the burden of preparation, and auditing fees, the supplier must bear.

Occasionally, companies will make unannounced supplier visits in instances where the supplier's actions have generated numerous red flags or the supplier has declined to fill out the self-assessment. And in extreme cases when a supplier has generated red flags and has not initiated improvement action, companies have terminated supplier relationships. Three Sustainable Market Leaders, on condition of anonymity, have told me they terminated at least one relationship under these circumstances within the past two years.

Supplier Business Performance Improvement Efforts. A value chain rich with healthy, profitable, diverse suppliers is good for the suppliers and the companies that employ them. After all, a healthy supplier reduces uncertainty; not only will the supplier have more to lose if it chooses to cut corners on its product quality, but it is less likely to go out of business. Healthy suppliers reduce supply chain turnover due to bankruptcy and promote the ability to plan long term with a modicum of certainty. In short, healthy suppliers are in a company's best interests.

Fortunately, many companies not only agree with this view but are dedicating resources to help their suppliers improve their business (as well as sustainability) performance. Some companies are providing training to suppliers; others are going so far as helping to increase suppliers' workers' satisfaction.

For example, Edna Conway, who directs value chain management activities at Cisco, proudly described her company's efforts to assist diverse suppliers' improve their performance and capabilities. Specifically, Conway shared a story of working with David Morgan, the CEO of DW Morgan, a transportation and logistics company:

There are four fundamental pillars of the value chain that are all equally important to us; supplier diversity is among those pillars. A couple years ago we created a three-tiered mentorship program for diverse suppliers. Our program has multiple levels. First, we invited mentee company leaders, on our tab, to participate in UCLA's Management Development for Entrepreneurs training program for executives. Second, we established mentoring relationships between the CEOs of select suppliers and senior Cisco executives. Third, we created an advanced partnership between Cisco executive mentors and mentee company leaders to examine one specific business solution of our mentee's choice which they wish to transform. Transformation could include new solution deployment, expansion of an existing solution or service, or tackling globalization.

In fiscal year 2010 we mentored DW Morgan, a diverse transportation and logistics supplier. The company has been a member of our supply chain for about a decade. They achieved such a degree of level of service that they were recipients of our Best Diverse Supplier Award for our 2002, 2005, and 2009 fiscal years. But if you ask them, up until last year they really struggled to deal with a wider audience. So in the advanced program (level 3) they decided, "We want a strategy to build a win in a variety of programs."

We selected a specific set of internal opportunities and helped DW Morgan analyze their capabilities, both strong and those which needed enhancement. We partnered with them to ensure they truly understood our future plans for our global logistics model. This allowed them to take on new tactical assignments for us in new geographic markets. Having learned our system, they applied their transport expertise and saw an opportunity. "We think we can consolidate your domestic U.S. trucking," they stated. We worked with them to implement their plan and they did exactly what they proposed. In fact, within six months

- DW Morgan saw an 54 percent increase in Cisco business.
- Cisco gained increased in inbound and outbound visibility and cost savings.

All this with zero breakage and zero defects-based packaging rejections by customers. Our customers have come to expect the very best from Cisco—if they see a ding in the box they send it back. With these kinds of results, our mentoring relationship with DW Morgan was a win for both of us.

I had the privilege to talk with David Morgan, CEO and co-founder of DW Morgan, after my conversation with Edna Conway at Cisco. Morgan and his wife Palmyra founded DW Morgan twenty years ago. Their company's initial business model was to "provide a better solution for customers who needed urgent-delivery, high-service shipping." Over time the company's focus has evolved to "solve the 'last mile' problem in manufacturing supply chain." Morgan used Cisco as an example client to describe the company's solutions:

It's relatively easy for a company like Cisco to put goods on a plane and send them to a factory or distribution center overseas. That's the original business we served, and it now has become a commodity service.

But what happens when the goods arrive in a manufacturing or distribution center? These are the places where traditional transportation and logistics providers broker local service to an outside company. And, they're where visibility, security, standard operating process, and reliability get hopelessly lost.

We have our own trucks, facilities, staff, and technology in place in all of these locations—more than a dozen offices around the world. And, we have a U.S.-based central management team to coordinate work between these offices. As a result, our clients get identical quality, coordination, and control, whether products are moving through Mexico, Malaysia, or Main Street, USA.

Morgan explained how the mentoring process worked:

Morgan joined the mentorship program a year ago, with an executive Cisco sponsor and another Cisco employee serving as DW Morgan's main coordinator. Our experience with them has been amazing. Though Morgan has worked with Cisco for ten years or more; up until this last year our success story has been one of the best-kept secrets inside the corporation.

In the past, every time Cisco gave us a challenge, we hit the ball out of the park for them. However, our work was confined to very specific groups and assignments. Our Cisco mentors helped us define our capabilities and tell our story to a broader Cisco audience. It was a very structured engagement, beginning with a review of our business, SWOT analysis, and a survey of our existing Cisco customers. Then they helped us identify our best new opportunities and gave us the platform to make our case for the business.

We had to go out and do the hard work of winning some key, new Cisco projects. The program wouldn't have worked if we didn't have the right quality, management, and price. But it's also true that we couldn't have accomplished this on our own, either. The mentorship program has been invaluable as an aid in understanding how to market our services within Cisco and getting the right messages to the right audiences.

Morgan's mentors helped the company refine their marketing messages, gain access to executive analysis approaches, identify areas of potential growth, and ultimately

over the course of the whole year, I think we've had approximately a doubling of revenue. And, some of our new business with Cisco has built strategic capabilities that have

helped us become more valuable partners to our other
customers.

As we will see in Chapter Eight, Cisco's diverse supplier
mentoring program is about mutually beneficial actions, not
altruism.

Conclusion

This chapter described how Sustainable Market Leaders are integrating sustainability into day-to-day operations. Sustainable
Market Leaders view their integration efforts as a two-way street:
their suppliers benefit from the hands-on training offered through
sustainable supply chain management efforts, and the Market
Leaders providing such training benefit from new ideas flowing
from their suppliers. The chapter discusses many of the ways
suppliers, employees, and other stakeholders boost Sustainable
Market Leaders' efforts to reach sustainability goals. The next
chapter raises the importance of metrics in the management of
companies' sustainability performance.

DIAGNOSTIC

Corporate Culture

Folded-Arm Syndrome

1. How would you characterize your company's willingness to listen to criticism from stakeholders?
2. When was the last time you brought a person outside of your company into one or more of your corporate or competitive strategy discussions?
   a. Was the person allowed to speak, or just listen?
   b. If he or she was allowed to speak, how would you describe the reaction his or her comments received? Did your company act on this feedback?

Lack of Apparent Connection Between Sustainability and the Drivers of Value Creation

1. If you asked any of your company's senior executives to describe your company's sustainability commitments, would they be able to? What would they say? Would their answers be consistent?
2. What if you asked your managers the same question?
3. Would your employees say that sustainability is a core value of your company? Would they mean it?

Innovation

Adjust Existing Processes

1. Has your company tied innovation ideas to the company's sustainability objectives?
   a. Does your company require all innovation ideas to have at worst a neutral impact on the environment?
2. Does your innovation process include the task of confirming that the issues of sustainability have been considered before any proposed innovation moves to the funding phase?

Participate in Open Sustainability Idea Exchanges

1. Do you look outside your organization for sustainability innovation ideas?
2. Would your company join an open sustainability idea exchange? If not, how would you describe the roadblocks to joining such an exchange?

3. Have you discussed sustainability innovation ideas, or at least sustainability challenges, with your peers or with other companies?

Crowdsourcing

1. Would you post a call for sustainability ideas online?
2. Would you be willing to provide funding to pursue one or more of these ideas?
3. Would you post an update on the progress of your sustainability crowdsourcing campaign, even if you didn't receive ideas that would make a difference?

Talent Management

1. How would you describe the sustainability-related training you provide to your employees?
2. If asked, would your employees report that your company has helped improve their sustainability knowledge or at least their awareness?

Finance

Investment Proposal Considerations

1. Has your company inserted a price for carbon emissions when considering investments in new hard assets?

Pricing Strategy/Assessing Financial/Environmental Impact Tradeoffs

1. Has your company considered approaches to integrate your lower carbon footprint into your pricing strategy to create a low-price competitive advantage?
   a. What would your company's reaction be to a competitor that pursues such a low-price advantage?
2. Has your company considered introducing a tiered pricing structure for customers, where the tiers are determined by the environmental impact of the approach you take to deliver value for your customer? (For example, if you use air freight to transport goods to your customer, they would pay a higher price driven by both the speed with which they receive their order and the additional environmental impact of using faster transport methods.)

Performance Management

1. Has your firm settled on a set of KPIs it uses to measure and report its progress against sustainability objectives?

2. Are environmental and/or social sustainability KPIs included in your CEO's performance metrics package that is regularly presented to the board?

3. Has your company enacted environmental impact (for example, carbon emissions, water consumption, waste to landfill) "budgets" for each business unit and/or department?

   a. Are managers held accountable for their performance against these budgets? For example, is a portion of a manager's compensation determined by his or her performance against environmental/social impact budget?

Business Development

Brand Management

1. Could you clearly and succinctly state what your brand stands for from a sustainability perspective?

2. Would your fellow executives give the same answer?

Ambidextrous Marketing: Reserved on the Outside, Vociferous on the Inside

1. In the past year, how often has your company been accused of greenwashing?

2. What percentage of your marketing campaigns emphasize your company's sustainability progress?

3. Relative to your peers, are you promoting your sustainability progress more aggressively or less aggressively?

4. From where does your sales force receive information on your company's sustainability progress?

   a. If asked, would each of your most prominent sales executives give similar, specific to your company sustainability, sales messages?

5. Would your most strategic accounts say your sales force has successfully communicated your company's sustainability progress to them?

Procurement and Supply Chain Management

Sustainable Procurement Policies and Procedures

1. Has your company enacted a sustainable procurement policy that clearly presents the environmental and social behaviors you expect from your suppliers?

2. Are procurement employees trained on the topic of sustainability and the company's sustainable procurement policies?

3. Have you integrated these environmental and social behavior guidelines into questions that are included in the requests for proposal you tender to potential suppliers?

4. Does a percentage of your supplier-of-choice decision depend on suppliers' responses to these questions?

Supplier Business Performance Improvement Efforts

1. Has your company enacted a supplier code of conduct?

2. In designing your supplier code of conduct, did you consider the burden your suppliers are under when suppliers operate under different codes of conduct issued by intra-industry competitors?

3. Does your company issue self-assessments to its suppliers so that suppliers can assess their compliance with your code of conduct?

4. Does your company grade these self-assessments in order to spot points of environmental or social indecency risk in your suppliers' operations?

5. Does your company follow up on these self-assessments with in-person audits of the suppliers presenting the greatest risk of noncompliance with your code of conduct?

6. Does your company provide suppliers with access to your company's sustainability experts in order to enable the suppliers to develop and execute noncompliance remediation programs?

7

ANALYZING AND
COMMUNICATING PERFORMANCE

A two-year journey reached the end of its first leg on April 20, 2010, when Hilton Worldwide unveiled a proprietary system called LightStay, which calculates and analyzes its hotels' individual and collective environmental impacts. The system measures energy and water use and waste and carbon output at Hilton Worldwide properties globally. LightStay analyzes environmental performance across two hundred operational practices, ranging from paper product usage to chemical storage.

Guided by pragmatism, Hilton Worldwide first planned and then thoroughly tested LightStay among 1,300 of its 3,600 properties before speaking publicly about its investment and its aspirations. The results of its internal tests clearly demonstrated LightStay's value and efficacy. In brief, the 1,300 properties that used LightStay in 2009 reduced their energy use by 5 percent, their water use by 2 percent, their carbon output by 6 percent, and their waste output by 10 percent. These reductions led to one more fungible result: a $29 million reduction in these properties' collective utility bills.

Convinced that transparency was the best path to external credibility, Hilton Worldwide commissioned a third party to audit and validate the results of Hilton Worldwide's analysis. Buoyed by this third-party verification, Hilton Worldwide decided to require each of its 3,600 properties worldwide to adopt LightStay and publicly announced the creation of and benefits derived from LightStay.

The LightStay development and subsequent announcement have benefited Hilton Worldwide in at least two ways. Because Hilton Worldwide was the first global hotel chain to require all of its hotels to adopt an environmental measurement system, the announcement differentiated it from its peers in the minds of individuals and institutions that apply sustainability criteria to hospitality service provider decisions. The second benefit was that many of the Hilton Worldwide hotels participating in the LightStay program earned an environmental credibility that got them listed on Travelocity's and Expedia's green travel websites.

As we saw in Chapter Two, suppliers' power relative to buyers' power has been reduced as more and more buyers have integrated sustainability within their codes that determine companies with which to partner. Without LightStay, and a related commitment to implement LightStay's environmental improvement recommendations at individual hotels, it is less likely that Hilton Worldwide would have been included among these green hotel listings.

Hilton Worldwide's story provides us with at least three insights into the strategic development and deployment of sustainability performance management systems:

1. The system can connect efforts to manage sustainability within a company with that company's departments. However, there's a fine art to crafting the most appropriate metrics to measure and report.
2. It matters how and when a company communicates its sustainability progress. Sustainable Market Leaders like Hilton Worldwide speak *after*, not *ahead of*, their data.
3. Sustainability performance measurement efforts can drive competitive differentiation and create tangible business value. This value can take the form of cost savings, competitive differentiation, or both.

The Fine Art of Crafting Sustainability Performance Systems

In their seminal book, *Competing on Analytics*, Tom Davenport and Jeanne Harris state that "there is considerable evidence that decisions based on analytics are more likely to be correct than those based on intuition."[1] Given the combination of stakeholders and the critical mass adoption of and trust given to opinions shared via social media, making "correct" decisions pertaining to energy and carbon emissions reduction initiatives has become ever more critical.

Yet making good sustainability decisions presents a more difficult challenge than most, if not all, preceding megatrends because there are so many metrics to choose from. Should a company measure its energy consumption in absolute or relative terms? If in relative terms, what year should the company employ as a baseline? What's to stop the company from choosing a year with abnormally high absolute emission levels? And so on.

As of late 2010, there are still few standards sustainability metrics that apply to many companies within the same industry, and fewer still that apply across industries, but there are successful pockets of cross-competitor collaboration in creating standards. Consider, for example, the U.S. online travel agents market. In this industry, competitors agree on the importance of encouraging and enabling travelers to choose "green hotel" travel options. And what defines a green hotel? This is the question Alison Presley at Travelocity faced when she realized that a standard definition was required in order for her company's Travel for Good program to gain traction:

> When we decided to flag green hotels on our site, we immediately faced the question "What *is* a green hotel?" At that time, there was no agreed-upon industry definition. We worked with the United Nations and a group of nonprofits and NGOs [nongovernmental organizations], and even our

competitors to form the Global Sustainable Tourism Council, and together we defined what it meant to be a sustainable hotel. The standard that came out of this process was named the Global Sustainable Tourism Criteria.

Sustainable Market Leaders themselves are still refining the metrics they employ to measure sustainability performance, and acquisitions and divestitures continually alter the geographic and consumer markets within which they compete. But all companies can learn from the straightforward approaches they have employed thus far to developing performance metrics.

Tracking sustainability requires a full set of metrics to be tracked internally and a subset to be reported externally.

Metrics for Internal Measurement

Dan Cherian, whose initial work at Nike also included the integration of sustainability performance metrics with the company's internal scorecards, acknowledges the difficulty of developing internal measurements:

> Establishing sustainability performance metrics is a very complex topic. It has to be customized to how your company measures performance overall as well as how it perceives sustainability. We spend endless hours trying to work it out because it is not an exact science right now. There is not really a global agreed upon standard on how companies should measure sustainability internally. Internal performance management is quite complex. Most business units resist adding another metric to their already bulging scorecards. It can be done but needs a lot of prep work, conversations, and patience.

Developing and using internally reported metrics is complex in part because of the wide range of dynamics to consider, including

- The challenge of "rolling up" regional metrics into global metrics
- The challenge of "rolling up" facility-level metrics into regional metrics
- The accessibility and reliability of certain data points
- The lack of resources to investment in the development or licensing of a sustainability performance measurement system
- Resistance among business units and other departments to add metrics to the established list of success (and remuneration) metrics

I wish that I had a good way to simplify the task. What I can do here is relay advice on tactics from a few interviewees:

- Several companies reported starting with the set of issues their materiality assessment (as described in Chapter Three) identified as highly important.
- Others said they looked at peers' sustainability efforts, leveraged the questions included in proposal requests they received, and used metrics from scorecards issued by global and influential companies to their suppliers. Indeed, numerous companies confessed off the record to studying competitors' reports for inspiration.
- Six Sustainable Market Leaders said they augmented their metrics with metrics queried in one or more questionnaires included in tender processes in which they participated.

Perhaps the more significant source of ideas will be intra-industry collaboration like that of the online travel agents' market described earlier.

Metrics for External Publication

Pockets of standards and guidance already exist to guide which metrics to publish externally. Consider the Global Reporting

Initiative (GRI). Ceres, the Boston, Massachusetts, nonprofit working with companies and investors to address sustainability challenges, founded GRI in the late 1990s to develop a framework for reporting a company's sustainability information. During the past decade, reliance on the GRI reporting protocol has grown from twenty stalwart companies in 1999 to nearly 1,400 companies in 2009.

The Carbon Disclosure Project (CDP) has similarly progressed. Established in London in 2000, the CDP has used its annual survey to collect a deep global repository of companies' greenhouse gas emissions and climate change strategies. Much like the GRI, participation in the CDP has steadily increased from 235 companies in 2003 to nearly 2,500 companies in 2009.

The separate existence of, and interplay between, the GRI and the CDP has occasionally led to metrics confusion. But in July 2010 they jointly issued a "linkage document" that demonstrates alignment between their two reporting protocols. For example, question EN18 in the GRI reporting guidelines asks companies to disclose "initiatives to reduce greenhouse gas emissions and reductions achieved." The CDP question 9.7 asks for similar information: "Emission Reduction Activities: Please use the table below to describe your company's actions to reduce its GHG emissions." The linkage document puts these two similar questions together on one page and provides clarifying comments that better explain what each methodology does and doesn't want included in response to these questions. So there are signs that standards are emerging.

In the end, sustainability performance management remains more art than science. But the forces shaping performance management and reporting are converging. These forces include Sustainable Market Leaders' desire to continuously improve, standard bearers codifying alignment between their protocols, and megacompanies like Wal-Mart, Procter & Gamble (P&G), and IBM tirelessly working to improve their sustainability performance in part by raising their partners' games. Ultimately such convergences will lead to an effective, if not efficient, mosaic of sustainability performance management standards.

When and How to Communicate Progress

While there is still great confusion about *what* to measure, there is a bit more clarity about *how* and *when* to communicate sustainability progress externally. At the time of writing, companies are not legally mandated to report their sustainability progress and performance. But competitors' actions, stakeholder requests, consumer doubts about the private sector's truthfulness, and government agency directives such as the Securities Exchange Commission's climate change directive are combining to create a proxy for such a legal mandate.

Sustainable Market Leaders resist the temptation to speak ahead of their data. Through experience or observation, these companies have concluded that the most effective way to avoid accusations of greenwash is to have the data that supports their environmental and social claims.

When these companies do announce data-backed updates on their progress, they thereby put pressure on their competitors, pushing them into uncomfortable positions. To wit, consider United Parcel Service's (UPS) efforts to improve their performance within a specific human rights issue, as recounted by Lynnette McIntire:

A good example of how embracing sustainability is helping us from a competitive position is the human rights campaign. We had a really lousy score when we first got involved with that on gay rights, lesbian rights issues. And we looked at ourselves in the mirror and talked to them and said, "Oh well, you know what? We need to do something." After embarking on an improvement campaign we earned a 100 percent score, which we've maintained for the last three years. Improving our performance in a transparent fashion then put pressure on our

competition, including one company that will not have those
rights until 2012 and is being scrutinized as a result.

Whether intended or not, Hilton Worldwide, UPS, and
other Sustainable Market Leaders' practice of speaking after their
data leads stakeholders to wonder what other companies in the
same markets are doing about the announced issues. The resultant chain of events leads competitors to choose between two
undesirable options: either make an announcement before they
have complete data to support it or remain silent until they have
data to speak about.

In addition to press releases, companies communicate their
sustainability progress to the outside world through questionnaire responses and sustainability reports.

Questionnaire Responses

Survey fatigue can be a problem for Sustainable Market Leaders.
One way to take that problem in hand is to think of survey
questionnaires as a chance to show pride (and exercise one's
bragging rights!). Said UPS's McIntire:

> Sustainability questionnaires push us to answer questions we
> don't particularly think we want to! We respond to 120 of
> those a year. There is somebody on my team who is primarily
> focused on responding to information requests.
>
> We think it's worth it to respond to surveys because we use
> it as a change agent and as a benchmarking exercise. So that's
> how we justify doing it. We want to educate people on who we
> are, what we do, and why we do it.
>
> It's also an ego booster. We use our responses competitively.
> We use those accolades competitively but also internally. It's a
> huge pride builder. It really helps to get people to stay engaged
> with sustainability in their own jobs if they can see that their
> efforts have made it possible for UPS to be number one on

Fortune's most admired in social responsibility. You feel like they're a part of it.

Sustainability Reports

Let's consider questions of frequency, medium, and content.

Frequency and Medium. Companies need to decide how often to communicate sustainability progress and what medium to use. The second decision is the more difficult.

Early predecessors of today's sustainability reports, focused on environmental, health, and safety issues, began to appear ten to fifteen years ago. These reports were paper based and were issued annually. Data populating these reports was nearly always manually collected and usually documented in emails and loose spreadsheets. The process of gathering the necessary data, let alone creating the prose around the information, was cumbersome and time consuming.

As depicted in Figure 7.1, Sustainable Market Leaders are reporting more frequently now than in the past, especially on their websites.

Many Sustainable Market Leaders still see value in publishing annual, paper-based reports. Consider the rationale behind paper-based, annual sustainability reports at Wesfarmers. One of Australia's largest firms, Wesfarmers is a retailer, energy, and industrial products company. Given its diverse range of businesses, Wesfarmers is in contact with a wide range of procurement executives. Increased interest in better understanding potential partners' sustainability commitments has increased the value of annual reports. According to Cameron Schuster, sustainability manager at Wesfarmers:

> Many contracts now from large organizations in Australia
> require the potential supplier to document their credentials in
> the area of sustainability. One of the ways that our businesses

Figure 7.1 Progression of Sustainability Reporting to Quarterly Online Reports

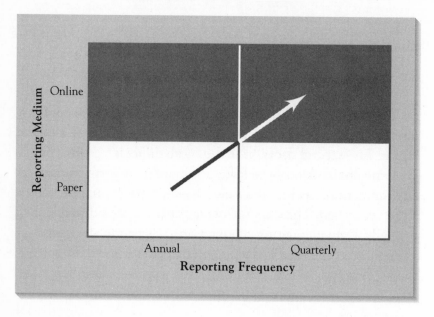

do this is with our sustainability report. Some of our divisions use the sustainability reports, in association with our annual financial report, quite often with their tender documents to address supplier's questions on social, environmental, economic, and governance issues. . . . The document almost pays for itself because it means these divisions do not have to go and reinvent the wheel.

But more and more companies are reporting online. Ben Packard at Starbucks recounted the decision to move from paper-based reports to online sustainability performance reports:

We have been doing the reports for nine years. We moved to online reporting two years ago. Our transition to online was spurred by a finding that readership of our paper-based reports was quite low. More importantly, we found out our own people were not reading the paper reports and did not know the key points that were in there.

Moving to an online report has several advantages for both the company and stakeholders. The burden of producing the 70 to 200 grammatically and pictorially polished pages that comprise the traditional sustainability report is being lifted from the overtaxed shoulders of sustainability managers. In their stead is a set of data-driven tables on topics ranging from tons of carbon emissions to the number of suppliers audited in a given year.

The aggregation of this data makes year-on-year comparisons easier for stakeholders, serving to inform their opinions about the companies they most closely examine. Increasing the amount of data available for stakeholders to review is one of the reasons Centrica transitioned away from annual, paper-based reports, as recalled by Amelia Knott. "Simply put, we can put more online than we can put in a paper report."

Sustainable Market Leaders are also moving to quarterly sustainability news releases. Part report, part press release, these quarterly updates often take the form of brief but slick postcards touting the company's progress and findings. Usually these communiqués include an interview with a senior executive coupled with a story of a client win earned on the basis of the company's progress to date.

These news blasts, usually emailed, for now strike me more as an effort to enhance brand and less an effort to transparently communicate with stakeholders. But a move to integrate more measures, reported on a quarterly basis, into these emails would increase their usefulness and trustworthiness.

I believe that ultimately annual sustainability reports will be replaced by two vehicles. First, much of the sustainability progress and risk information found in these reports will wind up in companies' financial reports. Indeed, the U.S. Securities Exchange Commission (SEC) issued a directive in February 2010 that public companies must disclose the risks of business disruption brought about by climate change in their financial reports. Second, quarterly online reports will provide the content needed for companies and stakeholders to engage in more frequent, and potentially less time consuming, conversations about ways companies can enhance their sustainability performance.

Content. The question of what content to include in an annual or more frequent sustainability report is most effectively answered by two straightforward questions: Who is the intended audience for the report, and what messages does the company want the report to communicate? 3M gives its answers to these questions in a document on their public website titled *3M Sustainability In-Depth: Defining Sustainability Report Content:*[2]

> 3M's Sustainability Report is the company's primary mechanism to communicate its sustainability policies, programs, and performance to its stakeholders. Therefore, defining the report's scope and content is extremely important. 3M uses the following key information sources to help define its report's content:
>
> 1. 3M's sustainability issue materiality determination
> 2. 3M's stakeholder interest evaluation
> 3. Direct feedback from users of previous Sustainability Reports
> 4. The Global Reporting Initiative sustainability reporting guidelines

Sustainability Performance Management Can Drive Business Value

The Hilton Worldwide LightStay story presented at the beginning of the chapter showed the business value of measuring sustainability performance. This value is not confined solely to immediate monetary benefits. The true value comes in the form of a deep understanding of the actions required for, resources consumed by, and lives and livelihoods altered by the creation and consumption of each saleable product or service. This understanding and the commitment it demonstrates make the difference between a sustainability strategy that leads to competitive advantage and one that may, indeed, be little more than greenwash.

Nike provides an illuminating example of the concept of demonstrated commitment. Long focused on the environmental impact of its products, in 2005 Nike formed an internal group called the Considered Design team. The group focuses on infusing considerations for the environment into the company's vaunted design processes. The Considered Index, introduced in September 2007, is now essential to Nike's product design processes. According to Nike:

> The Index is a tool for evaluating the predicted environmental footprint of a product prior to commercialization. In order for a product to be Considered, it has to be considerably more sustainable than the average Nike product. To measure this, we've created the Nike Considered Index.
>
> The index metrics are based on more than a decade's worth of research about materials, solid waste, innovations, treatments, and solvent use. They are also based on the evaluation of every commercial material used to manufacture Nike products using a life cycle approach. Products are assigned a "Considered" score using the Index framework based on Nike's known footprint in these areas. Only products whose score significantly exceeds the corporate average can be designated as "Considered."[3]

Although Nike's proprietary Considered Index is intellectual property that provides the company with a competitive advantage, Nike has a bigger goal in mind: to design and deliver products that use only recycled materials in perpetuity. Demonstrating the ethos of "co-opetition" (covered in Chapter Two), on

November 30, 2010, Nike shared its Considered Index, called the Environmental Apparel Design Tool, with its peers.

I end this chapter with two more specific contexts in which measuring sustainability performance enhances the effort: identifying best practices and finding opportunities to improve a product.

Identifying Best Practices

With factories spread across multiple locations, gathering the environmental and social impact data needed to calculate sustainability performance metrics is challenging. The measures used can vary by factory. Getting the data on impacts such as energy consumed, water consumed, and the like often requires gathering monthly utility bills, identifying the right measures, and manually documenting this information.

Even if the measures are consistent across factories, and the data are consistently gathered and documented accurately, there is one more challenge: how to capture and transmit the data to the team (or individual) responsible for calculating sustainability performance metrics at the enterprise level. I have heard many stories about "dirty spreadsheets"—spreadsheets sent from individual factories that don't neatly line up with one another—as well as vague phone messages with unverifiable data point reports.

Sensing opportunity, several software firms have developed environmental management programs to make the data-gathering, analyzing, and reporting process smoother, less manual, and more accurate. Putting aside the issue of expense, these systems can be quite valuable to the companies that choose to implement them. One rationale for making this investment is that the ability to identify best practices that lead to cost savings and reductions in environmental impact is enhanced.

Consider a company with factories across the United States. The company could use the system to gather and analyze environmental impact data, using standardized metrics, across all factories. Once equipped with this data, the company can then calculate an average (individual factory data likely will need to be normalized for scale) for each tracked measure and then compare each facility to this average. The facilities that are significantly below the average environmental impact likely have learned and employed lessons to achieve their relative top performance. A study of these facilities might yield best practices that can be replicated throughout the company's portfolio of factories. Cost savings and lower environmental impacts might result from this effort to increase performance across the system.

Another way to identify best practices via sustainability performance metrics is by participating in networks that are sprouting up by providers of environmental management system software. Numerous carbon accounting companies have developed software solutions to help companies gauge their environmental impact at the aggregate or factory level. This benchmarking exercise, in turn, should lead to a series of "what if" and "how to accomplish similar results" questions that may yield actionable insights.

Identifying Product Improvement Opportunities Through Life Cycle Assessments

As defined by the European Environment Agency, a life cycle assessment (LCA) is the process of evaluating the effects that a product has on the environment over the entire period of its life. The process can lead to more efficient resource use and fewer liabilities. It can be used to study the environmental impact of either a product or the function the product is designed to perform.[4]

As with all analyses, the accuracy of the LCA depends on the accuracy of the data the process analyzes. Sourcing this data to conduct an LCA for just one product can be a challenge. After all, data are needed from all of the vendors that contributed in some way to the supply, transport, manufacture, packaging, use, and (potential) disposal of the product. Understandably, this process can be very expensive, as it heavily relies on manual intervention. Imagine the expense of having thousands of unique products.

Behemoth consumer packaged goods companies Unilever and P&G have been working through this massive undertaking for years. For example, Unilever has conducted LCAs for more than 1,500 products. The information gleaned from their individually conducted LCAs has provided each company with insights into the product design process. For example, P&G's LCAs have revealed that "the largest environmental impact occurs when consumers use the company's products."[5] This information has led P&G to adjust attributes of their products that enable consumers to conserve resources.

Conclusion

Sustainable Market Leaders are disciplined; they gather their facts and data before making claims about their sustainability progress. Their goal is to provide stakeholders with the most accurate picture of their sustainability performance. Their dedication to the art of measurement and communication earns them credibility and respect from stakeholders. In turn Sustainable Market Leaders use this respect as currency to barter for constructive stakeholder dialogue, which helps these companies sharpen and renew their approach to sustainability. Chapter Eight explains this interaction in more detail.

DIAGNOSTIC

The Fine Art of Crafting Sustainability Performance Systems

1. How does your company balance the desire to market its sustainability attributes with ensuring it has the necessary data to support its claims?

2. How would you describe the sophistication of your sustainability performance measurement system? What percentage of your annual IT budget is dedicated to developing and maintaining this system?

3. How would you compare the breadth and depth of your sustainability reports and communications with your peers' efforts? In what areas are your communications better? In need of improvement?

4. Have you considered moving from an annual sustainability report to either a biannual or quarterly report?

5. To what extent do you create your reports with your stakeholders' ability to easily find the information they want in mind? How could you help make extracting information from your communications easier for your stakeholders?

6. How often do you talk with your peers and other companies to test the effectiveness of your sustainability measurements versus their sustainability measurements? When was the last time you asked a stakeholder or advisor to provide you with an honest critique of your measures?

7. How much do you really know about the environmental and social footprint of each of your products? How much do your peers know about their products? And how often are you asked for product-specific sustainability information by your customers or business partners?

8

RENEWING SUSTAINABILITY EFFORTS

In Chapter Seven we learned that Sustainable Market Leaders invest considerable time and thought into how they measure and communicate their sustainability progress to stakeholders. These companies have learned they cannot rest on past success. They know that sustainability's challenges and opportunities change continually, influenced by regulatory changes, human-made and natural disasters, environmental constraints, and shifts in public sentiment, and so forth. Pressures arise from any number of places, affect any number of functions, and cause any number of new problems. This chapter shows how Sustainable Market Leaders are tapping into their relationships with stakeholders to consistently renew their sustainability approaches.

eBay Engages

San Jose, California–based eBay has recognized the power of embracing sustainability for business performance and success. As the following story, told by Annie Lescroart, senior manager of sustainability communications at eBay, shows, the company is actively engaging its employees and consumer community to shape the company's sustainability strategy:

> Our sustainability efforts originated from a group of employees who had no mandate and just self-organized a few years back. We have the blessing of being in Silicon Valley; there are a lot of people who are progressive thinkers and concerned about

environmental issues. So these employees got together and started to figure out projects that they could bite off that made eBay a greener company. So it started with really small things, replacing disposables with durables in the break rooms, and evolved into larger and larger projects. Over the course of a couple of years the projects became big enough to attract executive attention. The first big project was a solar installation that we put on the roof of our north campus in San Jose, California. The Green Team made the business case for it and sold it up the chain. It's important to recognize that this type of entrepreneurial approach of one employee having a great idea and selling it through the chain is the cultural norm here.

From there the Green Team evolved into a program that was aligned with our business, which is a program that derives from our community of users. There are 90 million active users on eBay. Once we had the employee program up and running, we were charged to think about the big issues full time. We looked out to our community and said, "What if we open this up to the community and what would that look like?"

So we publicly launched the eBay Green Team website (www.ebaygreenteam.com) in February 2009. Since then, we've been in listening mode. All of our communication channels like blogs, the website that we have, all of our social media channels help us engage in two-way dialogue with our community of, now, nearly 300,000 Green Team members. And the critical factor in our approach is that we are listening first. Consider ideas, wherever the ideas come from. We've been evolving our strategy and trying to figure out what our path forward is. We're doing it in a way that really takes into account the sentiment and the feelings of the users that are engaged.

Lescroart's story focuses on eBay's employees and community of users. More broadly, companies are turning to five types of relationships:

1. Employees
2. Customers and members of interested communities
3. Value chain partners
4. Competitors
5. Nongovernmental organizations

Relationships with Employees

As the eBay story suggests, talented and sustainability-passionate employees represent a fantastic resource into which Sustainable Market Leaders tap. Either on a volunteer or more formal basis, employees often serve as extensions of the core sustainability teams.

Consider Gap Inc., for instance. The company relies on a network of "global responsibility ambassadors" across all of its brands. These ambassadors are employees who, on a volunteer basis, help drive change within the brands individually. To date, that work has focused on the "greening" of both brands' head-quarters building—eliminating waste, increasing recycling and composting, and enhancing employee education around living and working in a more sustainable fashion.

Getting Employees Involved

Employees often serve as extensions of the core sustainability teams.

Later in this chapter we see how Sustainable Market Leaders are looking to their communities of customers and separate but related groups of interested citizens for ideas and support. One question these companies need to answer is how to sift through the responses they receive from these communities. Companies are turning to their employees to take on this role, usually on a volunteer basis. Given the volunteer nature of this task, this solution is sustainable only when the employees themselves are passionate about sustainability. Alison Presley from Travelocity explains:

> Every quarter, since 2006, we give away two $5,000 volunteer vacation grants to consumers. They apply online. The employees actually donate their time to score the essays and then the ones with the highest scores wins.

So how do Sustainable Market Leaders source such passion, advice, and volunteer time from their employees? One way is to show employees that their senior leaders truly care about their ideas. Perhaps the best example of this comes from British Telecom (BT). A couple of years ago the company's BT Americas division ran an employee competition to find ideas to make BT more sustainable. Kevin Moss, head of corporate responsibility at BT Americas, shared this story with me:

> We wanted to invigorate our corporate responsibility work in the region. We were looking for ways to engage employees. Along with the president of BT America, I decided to hold a competition for the best sustainability ideas from employees. The first prize was a $500 donation to the charity of choice of whoever came up with the best idea. We did not promise to implement the idea, but it generated a lot of interest nevertheless. We had about sixty ideas from our workforce in the USA, which at the time were about 2,000 people. We put a team together to evaluate the submissions and recommend a winner to the president, who made the ultimate decision. He enthusiastically announced the competition on his monthly all-hands call and announced the winner with great fanfare on a successive all-hands call. The winner was a proposal to build a solar installation; and the second place, and I think it was $200 for the second place, was somebody who came up with a proposal to launch a carbon impact assessment service.
>
> The program was a success. Employees were still sending me ideas after the competition was finished because by then

they knew that the president was interested in their participation. I think there were a couple parts of the initiative that made it work so well. Firstly that we held it as a competition, and secondly that the president personally and prominently associated himself with it. He said he'd be picking the winner. And he then announced the winner. So the competition received a halo effect–like benefit from being associated with our top executive in the region.

So the idea that won was an innovative solar installation project at what was then our headquarters in El Segundo CA. The employee who proposed the project won because he put a load of work into his proposal. He did a lot of research. His proposal included a mini-business case. Along with a projected price, he calculated the energy savings we could recognize from this project. He also researched and documented the rebates that we can get together with a detailed timeline. He combined passion and thoughtfulness to create a winning proposal. The project was built and remains a showpiece of BT's commitment to renewable energy. It turned out that the idea of the second place proposal was already being considered in the company, but as a result of the interest generated by the competition, the US became the first country in BT outside of the UK to launch it.

Every company has one or more employees who are passion-ate about sustainability. Those individuals want to have personal impact. Connecting them with an appropriate set of company resources is in the best interest of all parties. Employees will feel more valued, and the company's sustainability performance will likely improve as a result.

Relationships with Customers and Interested Communities

Each of us wears many hats, perhaps as parent, student, teacher, employer, employee, consumer, and concerned citizen, just to name a few. Whatever hat we are wearing—personal or professional—most people can still relate to sustainability issues in their lives.

The "many hats" factor has intensified as masses of humanity have adopted the new social media. If a person sees an article on food shortage in sub-Saharan Africa that they want to share with others, they can blog about it, post it on Facebook, or simply send a tweet with a link to the article. I haven't seen scientific evidence of this yet, but I strongly suspect that the act of sharing a view online and receiving even just one positive response from someone else in return has strengthened individuals' beliefs that their opinions matter. As a result, social media–savvy individuals who are passionate about sustainability need only an invitation and a guiding question to get them to pitch in.

Like eBay, more and more Sustainable Market Leaders are reaching out to their customers and separate but related groups of interested citizens for ideas, advice, and support. For examples, consider also General Electric (GE) and Travelocity.

GE certainly understands the innate power of sustainability, passionate individuals, and social media. In July 2010, the perennial blue-chip company, along with four well-known venture capital firms, publicly announced the "GE ecomagination Challenge." Open to anyone and everyone, the challenge is a competition that seeks "to jump-start new ideas and deploy them on a scale that will modernize the electrical grid around the world."[1] GE and its four partners—Emerald Technology Ventures, Foundation Capital, Kleiner Perkins, and Rockport Capital—have dedicated $200 million to fund the winners' ideas.

To further tap into the wisdom of interested crowds, in July 2010 GE set up a website to which ideas could be submitted and commented on by the online public. Between July 13 and September 30, 2010, more than 3,700 ideas were submitted; collectively these ideas garnered more than 70,000 comments from nearly 70,000 registered users.

At Travelocity, participation in the company's volunteer vacation grants program works both ways. Not only are employees counted on to evaluate consumers' proposals for grants, but employees themselves can win volunteer vacation grants, too. And who gets to choose the employee winner? Travelocity's consumers. As Alison Presley explained:

> Every quarter we also give one $5,000 voluntourism grant to an employee. They apply online, submitting essays about their history of service and background, and then we ask past *consumer* winners to vote on their applications. We figure, "Who would be a better judge than the passionate people who already won the grants?" The voting process is blind of course. They can't see the employee's name or information and it creates a really interesting synergy between the external contest and internal contest, between our consumers and our employees. Since 2006 we've given away forty $5,000 volunteer vacation grants and we've sent people all over the world.

Relationships with Value Chain Partners

Value chain partners can be excellent sources for information, insight, and inspiration. In Chapter Six I described Cisco's supplier mentoring program and highlighted DW Morgan, the transportation management company that has won numerous supplier awards with Cisco. The mentoring relationship not only helps DW Morgan but benefits Cisco too. By working with DW Morgan, Cisco has gained new insights into the whereabouts of its inventory on a minute-by-minute basis and has saved a not insignificant amount of money on its transportation expenses in the process.

There is at least one hidden benefit of turning to your value chain partners for support with your sustainability strategy. These companies typically work with multiple clients that are trying to figure out their own solutions to their sustainability challenges.

Without breaking confidentiality, your value chain partners are likely well equipped to provide you with insights into how other companies have addressed vexing problems. But you will never know unless you start treating your value chain partners as trusted partners, not just vendors.

Sustainable Market Leaders have adopted this view. They frequently ask their value chain partners to participate in sustainability strategy discussions. Indeed companies such as Procter and Gamble (P&G) have installed supplier sustainability panels that regularly bring suppliers together to discuss common challenges and opportunities. In P&G's case, they worked closely with their Supplier Sustainability Board, consisting of more than twenty suppliers, over eighteen months to develop the company's Supplier Environmental Sustainability Scorecard.[2]

As we saw in Chapter Seven, sustainability performance information is a critical ingredient to making effective business decisions. By consulting with a sample of its value chain partners in the design of the company's environmental sustainability scorecard, P&G accomplished two things. Not only did it initiate a process to gather more information about its value chain partners' efforts and impacts, it also made its suppliers feel more like partners. One never knows when the goodwill associated with treating others as partners will come in handy.

Relationships with Competitors

More and more frequently, Sustainable Market Leaders are concluding they can't ensure our planet's sustainability—let alone their own—by themselves. But decades upon decades of competing for revenue, talent, and investor attention still lead even the most collaborative companies to continue going it alone.

Sustainable Market Leaders in industries ranging from chemicals to high technology to financial services have come to see the viability of working with competitors toward certain ends. One of the earliest (founded in 1992) examples of competitors collaborating for the common good is Responsible Care, the chemicals industry's voluntary initiative to improve environmental, health, and safety (EHS) performance of their products and processes. Through a participating network of fifty-three national associations, staunch competitors commit to identify and share best EHS management practices and operate openly and transparently with stakeholders. Essentially participation by such a large group of competitors (representing 90 percent of global chemical production) serves to keep competitors on this path of selective collaboration. Also, industry self-regulatory efforts are meant to help shape, if not decrease the need for, multilateral governmental oversight of and regulations for the industry.

Competing companies can collaborate on other issues, too. Companies in the high-technology industry rely on many of the same suppliers. Many of the best this industry has to offer have enacted supplier codes of conduct, which are documents that spell out the behaviors to which they expect their suppliers' adherence. The problem—one that heightened the need for supplier risk management efforts—was that these codes of conduct differed by company.

Imagine you are a supplier, perhaps based in a developing country. You operate at single margins, wholly reliant on scale to drive profitability. Within a two-year period, three of your largest customers visit you to discuss their expectation that you will sign to and adhere with their supplier codes of conduct. Implied in the discussion is that if you don't, then you will be subject first to onsite audits, then remediation plans, and finally dismissal from their supplier programs. Of course you decide to do everything you can to comply. But you now have three, or five, or eight, of these codes of conduct that are consistent about their higher-level expectations (for example, no incidents of child labor or corruption) but diverge on finer matters. So you are faced with a choice of either adding steps to your processes— further complicating your operations—or risk losing business.

Seeing this issue unfold, intense competitors such as HP, Dell, and IBM jointly formed in 2004 the Electronic Industry Citizenship Coalition (EICC). The EICC provides a set of responsible business practice guidelines for common suppliers, covering labor, health and safety, environment, management systems, and ethics. To further standardize the code of conduct process for suppliers, the EICC also puts forth tools to audit compliance with the EICC's code and helps companies report progress.[3]

Relationships with Nongovernmental Organizations

Sustainable Market Leaders are also molding mutually beneficial relationships with nongovernmental organizations (NGOs) that go far beyond corporate philanthropy. The ongoing partnership between Marks & Spencer, the giant British retailer, and Oxfam provides one such example. In return for bringing unwanted clothing to a local Oxfam shop, including at least one Marks & Spencer–branded clothing item, customers receive a coupon for £5 that can be used toward purchases of £35 or more at Marks & Spencer stores (the coupon must be used within one month of issuance). The arrangement is designed both to raise money for Oxfam's social work and to reduce the one million tons of clothing sent by the public to landfill in the United Kingdom each year.[4]

Oxfam sorts the clothing and either resells the clothing in their shops or sends the clothing to its recycling plant, where the clothes become materials for new clothing. Oxfam uses the profits from the sale of clothing to fund its charitable operations worldwide. As of June 2009, more than 600,000 consumers brought 3 million clothing items to Oxfam shops. Oxfam has used the clothing to raise more than £1.8 million for their overseas development work.

Though I was unable to gather quantitative evidence, I believe that Marks & Spencer derives at least three benefits from the arrangement:

1. It gains a way to strike deeper ties to consumers, especially those who are sustainability conscious. Some percentage of the 600,000 consumers who have participated to date are likely to be, at best, previously infrequent Marks & Spencer consumers. In a whimsical yet serious effort to deepen these connections, the retailer is using social media to encourage consumers to hold "wardrobe interventions" for their "poorly dressed" friends, to increase participation in the program.

2. It gains good publicity.

3. It enlists support toward achieving the company's sustainability goals, as laid out in its sustainability strategy, entitled "Plan A." Goals such as reducing waste to landfill are being met not only by Marks & Spencer's efforts but also by a virtual network of consumers, indirectly working on the retailer's (and society's) behalf.

Sustainable Market Leaders and NGOs, once strange bedfellows, are crafting arrangements similar in spirit, if not in nature, to the one between Marks & Spencer and Oxfam. Kimberley-Clark is working with Greenpeace International to design and implement new fiber-sourcing guidelines within the company's procurement efforts. Wal-Mart and the Environmental Defense Fund continue to refine the retailer's sustainability strategy while broadening the strategy's impact within industry. Corporations receive much needed environmental and social expertise; NGOs receive funding and support to achieve their goals.

Each of these examples are takes on the old "You scratch my back, I'll scratch your back" philosophy of working relationships.

These relationships adhered to an imaginary but well-understood boundary: NGOs are nonprofits; their brands (and associated consumer trust) could be touched but not shared (or sullied, in the eyes of some) by a company for the purpose of marketing a product to consumers. As I described in Chapter Two, the partnership between Clorox and the Sierra Club that helped bring GreenWorks to market erased that boundary in 2008.

Nongovernment organizations have become more selective about the companies with which they partner. If your company has decided to pursue a relationship with one or more NGOs, keep in mind that the top NGOs will likely require proof not only of your company's commitment to sustainability but also of actions your company has already taken to achieve your sustainability goals.

In the process of reaching out to these helpers and supporters, these companies are becoming stronger, more flexible, more relevant, and more aware. They are positioning themselves to perceive, understand, and respond to the next business imperative regardless of the imperative's relationship to sustainability. The last chapter of this book reveals how.

Conclusion

It is already clear that a "Set-it-and-forget-it" approach to sustainability will fail. Sustainability's challenges and opportunities will continue to evolve. The danger of not partnering with stakeholders is that your company will be caught unprepared to act as sustainability evolves. This chapter provides proven lessons for partnering with stakeholders in order to continuously renew your approach to sustainability.

DIAGNOSTIC

Forming Partnerships with the Public Sector

Is your company

1. Working alongside government officials, or at least in concert with an intra-industry association, to shape emerging environmental and disclosure regulations?
2. Identifying and crafting mutually beneficial solutions to social challenges your company's competencies can address?

Forming Partnerships with Nonprofit Organizations

Is your company

1. Targeting an environmental or social aspect of sustainability that your company has set out to address?
2. Fashioning an arrangement with a nonprofit organization that can amplify your efforts to achieve your environmental or social goal? (Note that amplification is not limited to aligning efforts to pursue a common goal, such as the Marks & Spencer–Oxfam relationship. Amplification can take a simpler form: the nonprofit organization can provide timely expertise to spur or support one or more sustainability initiatives.)
3. Seeking to develop a "halo-effect" increase in the level of trust consumers place in your company as a result of association with a highly reputable nonprofit organization?

Forming Partnerships with Nongovernmental Organizations

Is your company

1. Targeting an environmental or social aspect of sustainability that your company has set out to address?
2. Fashioning an arrangement with an NGO that can amplify your efforts to achieve your environmental or social goal? (Much like nonprofit organizations, NGOs have developed expertise in particular aspects of sustainability. Amplification can come simply in the form of knowledge transfer from the NGO.)
3. Seeking to develop a "halo-effect" increase in the level of trust consumers place in your company as a result of association with a highly reputable NGO?

9

KEEPING SUSTAINABLE
AND AGILE

A business imperative is a new circumstance in the economic environment that requires radical changes in a business's operations at every level. If changes are not made, the business cannot continue to create value consistent with previous levels; in extreme cases, the business cannot survive. The first four post–World War II business imperatives—quality, business process reengineering, globalization, and the Internet—collectively and individually have driven great change in the way business creates value. Each has necessitated significant changes to core processes and methods of supply chain management. Each has driven and continues to drive economic growth. Each one, and the changes it ushered in, disrupted the competitive balance within industries and even across borders. Each has left an indelible mark on how companies conduct business.

This concluding chapter focuses on two things. First we look at what sets the fifth imperative—sustainability—apart from the previous four imperatives. The second focus area is how working with stakeholders now will enhance corporate agility. I begin with a brief chronicle of the previous four imperatives. From there I develop the idea that what makes sustainability different lies in a change *for whom* businesses must create value in order to continue to operate. Previously, investors and employees made up the core beneficiaries of companies' efforts. Now, sustainability elevates the role of stakeholders whose interests were earlier considered tangential to business. Society and the Earth writ large must now be co-beneficiaries of business activity along with investors. As we have seen:

- Local community leaders expect companies to provide value to (or, at minimum, not extract value from) the citizens living in the areas where a company's local operations are based.
- Nongovernmental organizations (NGOs) expect compensation for serving as guides through the jungle of regulations designed to protect people and the environment.
- Numerous governments levy fees on companies' carbon regulations as a lever to force companies to reduce their impact on the environment.
- Other stakeholder groups abound, with their own agendas and demands.

Stakeholders Emerge as Initiators of Imperatives

Over the course of the previous four imperatives, more and more stakeholders have become active influencers of business direction and decisions. That widening has led to a gradual rise of society itself as a meaningful stakeholder.

Quality

Western industry's quality imperative rose from the ashes of post–World War II Japan. Devastated by war and humbled by the Occupation, Japanese business leaders were eager to rebuild both their nation and their international presence. These executives believed it was essential they make Japanese goods more competitive on the world markets, which entailed removing the image of Japanese goods as cheap and shoddy. Not only did Japanese industry overcome their disadvantageously poor quality in international markets, but they turned high quality into their own strong competitive weapon.[1]

U.S. consumers' perspective of Japanese products had shifted by the late 1970s. Japanese companies captured share in numerous markets, including transportation (fuel efficient cars), consumer electronics (Sony Walkman), and technology (semi-conductors). Many U.S. industries suffered irreparable damage, resulting in significant and permanent job losses. Eventually U.S. companies recognized that the Japanese challenge was based on the superiority of Japanese products, and the international quality movement was on.

Western firms installed various quality management systems. By the early 1990s, quality control circles had been established, customer needs were being addressed, and ISO 9000 was launched. Also, the role of chief quality officer had been estab-lished to spearhead implementation of quality throughout the organization. As a result, U.S. companies stemmed their loss of market share.

Kaizen, Japanese for "improvement," and *Kanban* (literally "billboard"), continue to serve as fundamental components point of the Japanese commitment to quality. *Kaizen* refers to the task of all workers to continuously improve all business functions; no idea is too small. *Kanban* refers to a related activity: the empow-erment of shop floor workers to stop production by displaying a card, sign, or billboard if they notice a flawed component in their section of the manufacturing process.

Business Process Reengineering

Business process reengineering (BPR) can be viewed as either an offshoot of quality or (as I see it) a new imperative in itself. While industry's acceptance of BPR led to similar process improvement activities as quality, the spark, and the goal, behind each differ. Western firms adopted quality to answer Japanese companies' market share challenge. BPR was driven by a desire to improve profitability through systematically reviewing the processes, tasks, and activities companies employed to create and distribute value.

In 1990 two influential business thinkers introduced the concept of business process reengineering in separately created and published articles. Michael Hammer, a former professor of computer science at the Massachusetts Institute of Technology, published an article in the *Harvard Business Review* claiming the major challenge for managers was to obliterate non-value-adding work rather than using technology for automating it. Hammer's implication built on at least one aspect of the quality movement: companies should eliminate work that does not add value to their customers. Underscoring the reception with which BPR was to be met, Thomas Davenport advocated similar thoughts in a well received 1990 *Sloan Management Review* article.[2,3]

Business process reengineering boiled down to reviewing a company's business processes, starting with the question, "How would we design a process that delivered value to our target market, from scratch?" BPR was rapidly adopted by a huge number of firms; by one count, as many as 65 percent of Fortune 500 companies claimed either to have initiated reengineering efforts or to have plans to do so. Their rationale was to achieve renewed competitiveness, which they had lost due to the market entrance of foreign competitors, their inability to satisfy customer needs, and their insufficient cost structures.[4]

The customer's and society's ascent continued during the period of business process reengineering as companies designed processes intended to meet customer needs and interests.

Globalization

To me the widespread business use of the term *globalization* has always been a misnomer. Globalization implies companies establishing outposts in the far reaches of the globe. But outfits have been conducting business overseas for hundreds of years. Trading companies in the Western world had operations in India, Macao, and other previously exotic locales in the 1600s.

Globalization in the context of the 1990s had more to do with effective management of multinational organizations than it was about expansion into far-off regions. Local communities had their voices heard as companies recognized the need to customize goods sold in local regions as a path to growth. But customization implied complexity, which implied increased costs. Coming off the BPR imperative, companies were loathe to increase expenses, so they did the next best thing: seek ways to produce customized goods while lowering costs through employing cheap labor. Off-shoring was born.

Overseas production was not without its challenges. Companies needed to have local management stationed near their contract production facilities to ensure the quality and timeliness of production. Firms found themselves involved with local sociopolitical challenges. Perhaps most pertinent to sustainability, companies opened themselves up to external criticism of labor and environmental practices employed by their contract producers.

Companies installed a mix of local managers and headquarters managers to oversee local operations to address many of these challenges. Progressive companies dedicated considerable time and resources to install more flexible organization structures. Interactions with external stakeholders, such as NGOs served as one aspect of these more flexible structures. Through these external stakeholders, society began to have a larger voice in the actions of corporations.

Internet Revolution

It started with a lower-case *l*. Confirmation of receipt was followed by a lower-case *o*. The communication abruptly ended before the lower-case *g* was received. Leonard Kleinrock, the University of California-Los Angeles (UCLA) computer science professor who connected the school's host computer to one at Stanford Research Institute, described October 29, 1969's watershed activity: "So the very first message ever on the Internet was the very simple, very prophetic 'lo,' as in lo and behold."[5]

When Marc Andreessen developed the software that became Mosaic, his focus was on creating a better mousetrap to find and access information he suspected was available online. Did he do so with the vision of becoming a billionaire? Probably. But the birth of the Internet browser, much like the birth of the Internet itself, was sparked by innovators interested in testing their limits, not by billion-dollar corporations seeking new ways to compete or catch up to competitors.

The Internet revolution is the first contemporary business imperative in which society played a larger role in sparking the imperative than did business. We can clearly see society's role in furthering the breadth and depth of the Internet revolution. The reader likely knows at least one person who left school before graduation to join a promising startup company built to exploit the Internet in some way. Employees, perhaps for the first (but not the last, as we'll see) time felt a satisfying connection between their personal interests (that is, using the Internet to change something about the world) and their company's interests. Many companies, in turn, adjusted human resource policies to attract and retain bright young talent interested in shaping the Internet. And nearly every company established an online presence to interact with customers in a new way (though many companies kicked and screamed along the way. I remember working with a prominent financial services client who refused to put up a website for fear that "participation in this fad will cause irreparable damage to our sterling reputation").

Few foresaw the Internet's most lasting impact: the advent of social media. Society (and business) has become reliant on the instant and near-free connectivity provided by the Internet. Imagine going twenty-four hours without checking email, blogs, or your favorite sports websites. People are news junkies; the Internet has provided us a constant fix.

Social media has become both a thorn in companies' sides and a new tool for companies to leverage to modify consumer perception of companies' efforts and intentions. Activists have led social media–based campaigns to reduce executive compensation at several prominent companies in 2011 alone. On the flip side, companies such as GE (refer to the Crowdsourcing section in Chapter Six) have successfully employed social media to engage the general public in efforts to source sustainability ideas.

The Sustainability Era and Society as Stakeholder

History suggests that society has overtaken business as the "sparker" of business imperatives. Indeed, the sustainability movement has been ushered in by the broadest set of stakeholders to date.

Here I briefly trace society's role as primary spark behind sustainability. The clarion call to modern-day environmentalism came from Rachel Carson, renowned biologist, writer, and ecologist, who was gravely concerned about the adverse impact usage of DDT was having on the environment. Her research formed the backbone of 1962's *Silent Spring*, which concluded that DDT and other pesticides had irrevocably harmed birds and animals and had contaminated the entire world food supply.[6] The book's most haunting and famous chapter, "A Fable for Tomorrow," depicted a nameless American town where all life—from fish to birds to apple blossoms to human children—had been "silenced" by the insidious effects of DDT.[7]

Twenty-five years later Gro Harlem Brundtland, then Norway's prime minister, and her UN team, referred to as the Brundtland Commission, published *Our Common Future*. This seminal work introduced the concept of sustainability to the world stage by defining sustainable development as development that "meets the needs of the present without compromising the ability of future generations to meet their own needs."[8]

John Elkington, through his 1994 book, *Cannibals with Forks*, was the first to link sustainability and business in a compelling way by demonstrating that business has three bottom lines it must manage: economic (traditional financial bottom line), environment (Are a company's activities harming or helping the physical environment's health?), and social (Are a company's activities harming or helping improve conditions in the local communities in which they operate?).

Society's sustainability actors aren't limited to visionary thinkers. Employees have initiated countless grassroots efforts to help their companies make even minor positive changes to help embrace sustainability. The international community, first through the Kyoto Protocol and now through the actions in Copenhagen, is changing the rules within which companies operate. Local communities, their voices amplified by NGOs and social media, are having their voices not only heard by industry but are also having their collective will felt by the business community.

Even the youngest generation is getting into the act. How many children have asked their parents why they aren't doing more to ensure that tomorrow's world isn't a better place than today's world? My six-year-old asks me very insightful (and detailed) questions daily about oil spills and homelessness.

So with their voices amplified by social media, their sphere of influence growing, and the scope of global challenges requiring their constant and long-term attention, the likelihood that this broad set of stakeholders will spark and shape the next business imperative—*beyond* sustainability—is high (see Figure 9.1).

A Payoff in Agility

Change comes in many forms. Regulations alter the legal boundaries of operations. Disruptive innovations transform how value

Figure 9.1 Society's Likely Role as Initiator of the Next Imperative

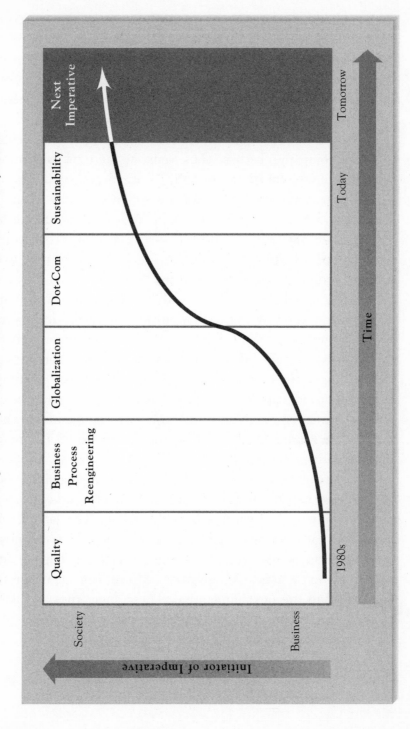

is created and delivered. New market entrants modify the competitive landscape. By embracing sustainability, Sustainable Market Leaders will detect clues about the next imperative before their peers. These companies have reached a critical conclusion: Industry has moved from a period of imperative as business benefactor to a period of imperative as sociopolitical benefactor.

Creating value for both investors and society presents a challenge for companies because these separate but now inseparable groups' interests are often quite different. In general, investors expect to earn returns from their investments, usually within a short period. Society expects kinds of "returns" that are harder to express in purely financial terms—such as zero carbon emissions and zero corruption incidents—and that might take five, ten, or even fifty years to materialize.

Society's level of engagement with business is likely to remain at the partner level. With this in mind, executives are developing virtual networks of social advisors to guide their companies both through the sustainability imperative today and the yet-to-emerge imperatives of tomorrow. These networks are enabling companies to increase the number of listening posts among society's constituents. These listening posts raise the likelihood that Sustainable Market Leaders will be the first recipients of emerging imperatives' earliest signals.

A company's agility relies not only on sensory capabilities but also response capabilities. Here again Sustainable Market Leaders have a competitive advantage over their peers. The same social networks that form Sustainable Market Leaders' listening posts can also serve as resources to provide expertise, guidance, and potentially extra hands as Sustainable Market Leaders transform to respond to the next imperative. These companies are likely to need to traverse only one learning curve in the face of the next imperative: the ins and outs of the imperative itself. Their peers will need to climb two learning curves: the ins and outs of the next imperative *and* the social networks that will likely play a critical role in sparking and shaping the challenges and opportunities to come.

While their peers have been wrestling with the decision to pursue sustainability, Sustainable Market Leaders have put themselves on a path to achieve a rare double play. Not only have these companies carved out competitive advantages today, but their swift and decisive actions have also positioned them for greater agility relative to their peers tomorrow. Their early adoption of sustainability has not only propelled their organizations up the learning curve faster and further afield of their peers, but their progressive actions have also led to relationships with the most visionary and influential stakeholders (leading NGOs, academics, local communities, and the like).

These stakeholder groups have both launched and colored the sustainability movement. These groups are likely to be the same influencers of the next imperative, regardless of its connection to sustainability. Sustainable Market Leaders have earned and secured access to these stakeholders' counsel. Whereas these companies will need only to traverse the next imperative's learning curve (with the benefit of counsel from the influencers of this subsequent imperative), their peers will need to work through at least two learning curves—sustainability (in part to earn relationships with these stakeholders) and the next imperative. So the additional activities adopted by Sustainable Market Leaders today will paradoxically make them faster than their peers tomorrow. Though sustainability's waters might evaporate, its impact will indeed be long lasting.

DIAGNOSTIC

Is Your Company Currently Capable of Being More Agile Through Integration of Sustainability?

1. Working with society to enhance your company's ability to sense and respond to new, society-driven imperatives.

2. Monitoring social media chatter about real or implied indiscretions within your value or supply chains?

3. Are you exposing your company to greenwash accusations by aggressively pushing the envelope on your sustainability claims?

Appendix A

RESEARCH METHODOLOGY

There were three main phases to my research on how many companies are connecting sustainability with their broadest corporate interests and what exactly they are doing.

Phase 1: Identifying Sustainability Among the 2010 Global Fortune 500

I started with the assumption that companies need to adapt their core strategy processes and policies for sustainability to become an essential ingredient of corporate and competitive strategy. To test whether companies are doing so, I analyzed the sustainability approach taken by every company on the 2010 Global Fortune 500 list. Specifically, I studied each company's website (including its sustainability micro site, as available), sustainability reports, annual reports, and articles for evidence of

1. Sustainability governance structures, including
   a. The vehicle used by each company's board to oversee the company's sustainability efforts
   b. Whether companies have sustainability working committees
   c. Whether companies have departments that manage sustainability centrally and regionally
2. Stakeholder engagement efforts regarding sustainability, including

    a. Stakeholder advisory panels, if any

    b. Employee engagement efforts

3. Supply chain sustainability management approaches, including

    a. Procurement policies to govern choice of suppliers based on suppliers' sustainability efforts

    b. Self-assessment, audit, training, and remediation efforts to ensure suppliers' sustainability performance at least meets expectations of all involved

Phase 2: Identifying Sustainable Market Leaders

I organized the 2010 Global Fortune 500 list into quartiles to identify companies to interview to better assess the link between sustainability and corporate strategy. To create these quartiles, I counted company listings on eight prominent sustainability indexes:

1. Global 100 Most Sustainable Corporations

2. Dow Jones Sustainability Index

3. FTSE4GOOD Index

4. Carbon Disclosure Project Leadership

5. Business Environmental Leadership Council

6. Business in the Community's Corporate Responsibility

7. Green Newsweek Rankings

8. Global 1000 Sustainability Performance Leaders

I assigned one point to each company every time it appeared on the most recent edition of each of the eight indexes. The highest score any company received was a seven out of eight. I termed the companies in the top quartile of companies on the basis of points "Sustainable Market Leaders." As I reviewed the range of publicly available information about each 2010 Global

Fortune 500 company, I logged all information about their strategy process adjustments. I then reviewed this information through three lenses: an intra-industry lens to identify best practices among peers, a regional lens to identify best practices among regional brethren, and a Sustainable Market Leaders lens to identify best practices of leaders among leaders.

Phase 3: Seeking Deeper Understanding of What the Leaders Do

I sought a deeper understanding of the connection between Sustainable Market Leaders and financial performance, driven by both competitive and corporate strategy processes. To get beyond the press releases and annual sustainability reports, I conducted more than one hundred interviews with Sustainable Market Leaders' executives—a total of more than three hundred hours of in-depth conversations. This book lets these leaders speak for themselves.

Companies and interviewees always responded politely to my requests, though some declined to be interviewed, citing either company policy or no available time. So I asked interviewees for suggestions of other companies to interview so that I could provide as accurate a picture of sustainability's business value creation potential as possible.

Where appropriate, I relied on my interviewees for sample best practices they use or admire in other companies. Sometimes the companies they cited were outside the scope of the Global Fortune 500. Indeed, some are midmarket; others are privately held. I reached out to several of these companies for insights, examples, and stories.

However, since my goal is to encourage and equip companies of all sizes and ownership structures to embrace sustainability as a means of improving innovation and performance, I thought it appropriate to include in this book some examples that, strictly speaking, fall outside the bounds of my formal research project.

Appendix B

INTERVIEWEES

This book would not have come together without the generosity of the following sustainability and strategy executives. Thank you for sharing your time, your insights, and your recollections with me.

Interviewee	Company
Tim Mohin	AMD
Julie Bisinella	Australia & New Zealand Bank
Eckhard Koch	BASF
Kevin Moss	BT Americas
Amelia Knott	Centrica
Edna Conway	Cisco
Mandy Knotts	Cisco
Mark Heintz	Deckers
David Morgan	DW Morgan
Annie Lescroart	eBay
Jorge Perez-Olmo	Gap Brand
Lisa Carpenter	Gap Inc.
Melissa Fifield	Gap Inc.
Kindley Lawlor Walsh	Gap Inc.
Frank Mantero	GE
Julia King	GlaxoSmithKline
Paul Murray	Herman Miller
Scott Carman	Hilton Worldwide

(*Continued*)

Interviewee	Company
Brian Larnerd	Hitachi
Charles Ruffing	Kodak
Chris Veronda	Kodak
Adam Elman	Marks & Spencer
Michelle Hamm	Monadnock Paper
Richard Verney	Monadnock Paper
Dan Cherian	Nike
Arlin Wasserman	Sodexo
Ben Packard	Starbucks
Peter DeBruin	State Street Global Advisors
Richard Pearl	State Street Global Advisors
Jean Sweeney	3M
Heather Tansey	3M
Alison Presley	Travelocity
Santiago Gowland	Unilever
Lynnette McIntire	UPS
Ed Rogers	UPS
Cameron Schuster	Wesfarmers

Appendix C

INTERVIEW PROTOCOL

I used a consistent approach for all of the interviews:

- I reached out, usually via email, to each interviewee to request permission to conduct an interview for my book.
- I emphasized that all interviews were "off-the-record." Permission from the interviewee and his or her company was required in order to publish content in this book.
- Interviewees were asked the same set of questions during the initial interview:
  a. Please introduce yourself (to learn more about the interviewee's role and remit, background, and so on).
  b. What does sustainability mean to your company— definition, business case, connection with corporate and competitive strategy?
  c. Has sustainability evolved into a dimension of competitive strategy between your company and your peers?
  d. How is sustainability connected with strategic planning? Are there specific tools, frameworks, or questions that are used during the strategic-planning process to ensure sustainability performance is considered and enhanced?

e. Sustainability management and governance—how is sustainability managed at your company? What kinds of adjustments has your company made to core value chain activities, to carry out your strategy?

f. Sustainability as a driver of growth, innovation, and agility—how have your company's sustainability efforts led to growth, innovation, agility, and so on?

g. How does your company employ sustainability measurements to both manage efforts and communicate impacts/risks/opportunities/progress to stakeholders?

h. How is your company engaging stakeholders, including employees, NGOs, and even competitors, to make as big an impact as possible and source ideas to further enhance your company's sustainability performance?

i. Are there one or more examples of internal processes that were adjusted to integrate sustainability into daily operations and business decision making?

j. Are there any diagrams that show redesigned processes, sustainability strategy tools, or the like that I can review and potentially reference in the book as best practices?

Notes

Foreword

1. World Commission on Environment and Development [WCED], *The Report of the Brundtland Commission: Our Common Future*. Oxford, UK: Oxford University Press, 1987, 1.
2. John Elkington, *Cannibals with Forks: The Triple Bottom Line of 21st Century Business*. Oxford, UK: Capstone, 1997.
3. Stuart L. Hart and Mark B. Milstein, "The Creative Destruction of Industries," *Sloan Management Review* 41:1 (Fall 1999).
4. Ram Nidumolu, C. K. Prahalad, and M. R. Rangaswami, "Why Sustainability Is Now the Key Driver of Innovation," *Harvard Business Review* (2009).
5. Christopher Meyer and Julia Kirby, "Leadership in the Age of Transparency," *Harvard Business Review* (April 2010).
6. Knut Haanaes and others, "First Look: Second Annual Sustainability and Innovation Survey," *Sloan Management Review* 52:2 (Winter 2011).

Introduction

1. World Commission on Environment and Development [WCED], *The Report of the Brundtland Commission: Our Common Future*. Oxford, UK: Oxford University Press, 1987, 1.

Chapter 1: Sustainable Companies Are Market Leaders

1. "Ahead of the Pack," *Wall Street Journal*, March 24, 2008.
2. See GE's ecomagination Fact Sheet. Retrieved November 4, 2010, from http://www.ecomagination.com.
3. Stephen Bernhut, "The Strategy Paradox—an Interview with Michael Raynor," *Ivey Business Journal*. Retrieved October 12, 2010, from http://www.iveybusinessjournal .com.
4. Ibid.
5. See p. 3 of the Carbon Disclosure Project Supply Chain 2009 Report. Retrieved October 26, 2009, from https://www. cdproject.net/.
6. See United Nations Global Compact. Retrieved October 26, 2009, from http://www.unglobalcompact.org.
7. Ibid.

Chapter 2: Sustainable Market Leaders Compete on Sustainability

1. The ISO 14001 standard requires that a community or organization put in place and implement a series of practices and procedures that, when taken together, result in an environmental management system (EMS). ISO 14001 is not a technical standard and as such does not in any way replace technical requirements embodied in statutes or regulations. It also does not set prescribed standards of performance for organizations. The major requirements of an EMS under ISO 14001 include a policy statement that includes commitments to prevention of pollution; continual improvement of the EMS leading to improvements in overall environmental performance; and compliance with all applicable statutory and regulatory requirements.

For more information, see the Voluntary Environmental Management Systems/ISO 14001 page on the U.S. Environmental Protection Agency's website. Retrieved October 13, 2010, from http://www.epa.gov.

2. Since the completion of *The Future of Value*, Santiago has accepted an offer from Nike to be general manager, Mobilize, which is a role in the company's Sustainable Business Innovation Leadership Team. I interviewed Santiago for this book in his Unilever role as vice president, Global Unilever Brand Development and Sustainable Development Strategy multiple times in late 2010 and early 2011. During his six years in the role, Santiago helped Unilever link sustainability with brand development and management strategy. He created the company's Brand Imprint process and implemented the Brand Imprint process in every one of Unilever's global brands and key categories. The Brand Imprint process systematically enables Unilever's brands to understand, manage, and enhance their impacts and connections with environmental and social issues. Santiago also developed the Unilever Corporate Brand strategy as part of Unilever's global marketing leadership team.

3. Michael Porter, *Competitive Strategy*. New York: Free Press, 1980.

4. Adam M. Brandenburger and Barry J. Nalebuff, *Co-opetition*. New York: Doubleday, 1997.

Chapter 3: Competing on Sustainability Creates Value

1. Chris Zook, *Profit from the Core: Growth Strategy in an Era of Turbulence*. Boston: Harvard Business School Press, 2001.

2. "Finding the Green in Today's Shoppers: Sustainability Trends and New Shopper Insights," Grocery Manufacturers Association and Deloitte, April 29, 2009.

3. See *The Greenhouse Gas Protocol Initiative: General Technical Accounting Questions*. Retrieved December 2, 2010, from http://www.ghgprotocol.org.

4. See *The UK Top 20 Retailers*. Retrieved December 2, 2010, from http://www.docstoc.com.

5. Carbon emissions are an expense in carbon regulated regions; a likely expense tomorrow in regions debating carbon regulation, including the United States.

6. "Report Shows How the S&P 500 Would Fare Financially Under Cap-and-Trade," *GreenBiz.com*. Retrieved December 30, 2009, from http://www.greenbiz.com/news.

7. Thomas Miner, "Wal-Mart Saves $3.5 Million with Slim Packaging," *Sustainable Life Media*. Retrieved December 30, 2009, http://www.sustainablelifemedia.com.

8. "Wal-Mart Is Serious ABOUT Going Green," *Green Chip Living*, September 25, 2009.

9. "AT&T to Plow $560 Million into Alt-Fuel Vehicles," *Sustainable Life Media*. Retrieved December 30, 2009, http://www.sustainablelifemedia.com.

10. "Wal-Mart Launches 5-Year Plan to Reduce Packaging." Retrieved July 7, 2010, from http://walmartstores.com.

11. Thomas C. Hayes, "Head Office of Hanover Bank Sold," *New York Times*, August 25, 1981. Available at http://www.nytimes.com.

12. Franz Fuerst and Patrick McAllister, "Green Noise or Green Value? Measuring the Price Effects of Environmental Certification in Commercial Buildings," *Henley Business School*, April 29, 2009. Available at http://hotellaw.jmbm.com.

13. Jonathan Low and Pam Cohen Kalafut, *Invisible Advantage: How Intangibles Are Driving Business Performance*. New York: Basic Books, 2002, 8.

14. See *Edelman 2009 Trust Barometer*. Retrieved September 25, 2010, from http://www.edelman.com.

Chapter 4: Crafting Sustainability Strategy

1. UPS Fact Sheet. Retrieved September 27, 2010, from http://www.pressroom.ups.com.

Chapter 5: Leading Strategy and Management Efforts

1. See GlaxoSmithKline's Corporate Responsibility Governance website. Retrieved October 14, 2010, from http://www.gsk.com.
2. See ANZ's Corporate Responsibility website. Retrieved February 8, 2010, from http://www.anz.com.
3. See ANZ's Corporate Responsibility Committee Charter. Retrieved February 9, 2010, from http://www.anz.com.
4. Ibid.
5. See Bayer's Sustainable Development website. Retrieved February 8, 2010, from http://www.sustainability2008.bayer.com.
6. Rick Merritt, "Apple Board Rejects Calls for New Environmental Efforts," *EE Times*. Retrieved February 8, 2010, from http://www.eetimes.com.
7. Robert Kropp, "Corporate Boards Taking Larger Role in Pushing Sustainability Agenda," *GreenBiz.com*. Retrieved January 19, 2010, from http://www.greenbiz.com.

Chapter 6: Embedding Sustainability into the Value Chain

1. Henry Chesbrough, *Open Innovation: The New Imperative for Creating and Profiting from Technology*. Boston: Harvard Business School Press, 2003.
2. See UC Berkeley's Center for Open Innovation website. Retrieved December 29, 2010, from http://openinnovation.haas.berkeley.edu.

3. See GreenXchange's website. Retrieved December 29, 2010, from http://greenxchange.force.com.

4. Eliyahu Goldratt and Jeff Cox, *The Goal: A Process of Ongoing Improvement*. Great Barrington, MA: North River Press, 1984.

5. Elisabeth Rosenthal, "Slow Trip Across the Sea Aids Profit and Environment," *New York Times*, February 16, 2010. Available at http://www.nytimes.com.

6. See Maersk Slow Steaming presentation. Retrieved February 17, 2010, from http://www.toysa.com.

7. Ibid.

8. "How National Grid Ties Executive Pay to Carbon Reduction," *Environmental Leader*. Retrieved February 17, 2010, from http://www.environmentalleader.com.

9. See Aviva's Supplier Policy. Retrieved February 15, 2010, from https://www.aviva.com.

10. See BMW's website. Retrieved February 10, 2010, from http://www.bmwgroup.com.

11. See Veolia's Sustainable Development website. Retrieved February 12, 2010, from http://www.sustainable-development .veolia.com.

12. See Volkswagen Supplier Relations Guide. Retrieved February 18, 2010, from http://www.volkswagenag.com.

Chapter 7: Analyzing and Communicating Performance

1. Thomas H. Davenport and Jeanne G. Harris, *Competing on Analytics: The New Science of Winning*. Boston: Harvard Business School Press, 2007, 13.

2. See 3M *Sustainability In-depth: Defining Sustainability Report Content*. Retrieved October 5, 2010, from http://solutions.3m .com.

3. See *Nike Considered*. Retrieved October 5, 2010, from http:// www.nikebiz.com.

4. See European Commission Environment Glossary website. Retrieved October 5, 2010, from http://ec.europa.eu/ environment.
5. See P&G's New Long-Term Vision Environmental Sustainability website. Retrieved October 5, 2010, from http://www.pg.com.

Chapter 8: Renewing Sustainability Efforts

1. See GE's July 13, 2010, press release. Retrieved October 1, 2010, from http://files.gereports.com.
2. "P&G Launches the Latest Supplier Sustainability Score-card," *GreenBiz.com*. Retrieved December 29, 2010, http://www.greenbiz.com.
3. See EICC's website. Retrieved October 1, 2010, from http://www.eicc.info.
4. See *M&S and Oxfam Clothes Exchange*. Retrieved December 29, 2010, from http://plana.marksandspencer.com.

Chapter 9: Keeping Sustainable and Agile

1. Robert E. Cole, *Managing Quality Fads: How American Business Learned to Play the Quality Game*. New York: Oxford University Press, 1999, 3.
2. Michael Hammer, "Reengineering Work: Don't Automate, Obliterate," *Harvard Business Review* (July/August 1990): 104–112.
3. Thomas Davenport and James Short, "The New Industrial Engineering: Information Technology and Business Process Redesign," *Sloan Management Review* (Summer 1990): 11–27.
4. See *answers.com*. Retrieved December 10, 2009, from http://www.answers.com.

5. Phillip Rosenbaum, "Web Pioneer Recalls 'Birth of the Internet,'" *cnn.com*. Retrieved October 29, 2009, from http://www.cnn.com.
6. Rachel Carson, *Silent Spring*. Boston: Houghton Mifflin, 1962.
7. See National Resources Defense Council. Retrieved December 20, 2009, from http://www.nrdc.org.
8. World Commission on Environment and Development [WCED], *The Report of the Brundtland Commission: Our Common Future*. Oxford, UK: Oxford University Press, 1987.
9. John Elkington, *Cannibals with Forks: The Triple Bottom Line of 21st Century Business*. Oxford, UK: Capstone, 1997.

Index